AUTOBIOGRAPHY OF JOHN STUART MILL

AUTOBIOGRAPHY OF
JOHN STUART MILL

PUBLISHED FROM
THE ORIGINAL MANUSCRIPT IN THE
COLUMBIA UNIVERSITY LIBRARY

WITH A PREFACE BY

JOHN JACOB COSS

COLUMBIA UNIVERSITY PRESS, NEW YORK

This book was reissued in 1944
as a memorial to
John Jacob Coss, 1884-1940
Moore Collegiate Professor
Columbia University

PREFACE

JEREMY BENTHAM, John Stuart Mill, and John Morley in their life dates cover the period from the middle of the Eighteenth Century to the present day. The American Revolution, the French Revolution, English Reform, and the World War are all included in these dates, as in the transformation of the Western World into a civilization predominantly industrial. Mill grew out of Bentham. Mill and Morley worked together for many years. All show that ability to combine great learning and scholarship with keen insight into contemporary affairs which has been one of the chief glories and ornaments of public life in England.

Mill's Autobiography shows, as few books can, the growth of a man in the midst of his age. In many ways it is primarily an account of the social history of England in the first three quarters of the Nineteenth Century. Yet it is the personal though dispassionate story of the conflict of an integrated spirit with ideas and with the affairs of men. One sees an age, and one sees a man; and both man and age are so a part of our own day that by knowing them we learn to know ourselves.

The text as printed in this volume has been taken from a manuscript of the Autobiography recently given to Columbia University by members of the Department of Philosophy. It has been considered desirable, as the definitive printing of Mill's own hand, accurately to follow the varying capitalization and punctuation of the manuscript, and in this form this version of the Autobiography is commended to its readers. It seems evident that this manuscript is the final draft intended for publication, because of the statement by Miss Helen Taylor, written by herself and attached to the manuscript, as follows:

"Autobiography of J. S. Mill written by himself. To be published without alterations or omissions within one year after my death.

HELEN TAYLOR."

The editorial work required was undertaken by Mr. Roger Howson, Assistant Librarian of Columbia University.

JOHN J. COSS

COLUMBIA UNIVERSITY
July, 1924.

A CHRONOLOGY OF MILL'S LIFE AND WRITINGS

JOHN STUART MILL

Chapter I

CHILDHOOD AND EARLY EDUCATION.

IT seems proper that I should prefix to the following biographical sketch, some mention of the reasons which have made me think it desirable that I should leave behind me such a memorial of so uneventful a life as mine. I do not for a moment imagine that any part of what I have to relate can be interesting to the public as a narrative, or as being connected with myself. But I have thought that in an age in which education, and its improvement, are the subject of more, if not of profounder study than at any former period of English history, it may be useful that there should be some record of an education which was unusual and remarkable, and which, whatever else it may have done, has proved how much more than is commonly supposed may be taught, and well taught, in those early years which, in the common modes of what is called instruction, are little better than wasted. It has also seemed to me that in an age of transition in opinions, there may be somewhat both of interest and of benefit in noting the successive phases of any mind which was always pressing forward, equally ready to learn and to unlearn either from its own thoughts or from those of others. But a motive which weighs more with me than either of these, is a desire to make acknowledgment of the debts which my intellectual and moral development owes to other persons; some of them of recognized eminence, others less known than they deserve to be, and the one to whom most of all is due, one whom the world had no opportunity of knowing. The reader whom these things do not interest, has only himself to blame if he reads farther, and I do not desire any other indulgence from him than that of bearing in mind, that for him these pages were not written.

I was born in London, on the 20th of May, 1806, and was the eldest son of James Mill, the author of the History of British India. My father, the son of a petty tradesman and (I believe) small farmer, at Northwater Bridge, in the county of Angus, was, when a boy, recommended by his abilities to the notice of Sir John Stuart, of Fettercairn, one of the Barons of the Exchequer in Scotland, and was, in consequence, sent to the University of Edinburgh at the expense of a fund established by Lady Jane Stuart (the wife of Sir John Stuart) and some other ladies for educating young men for the Scottish Church. He there went through the usual course of study, and was licensed as a Preacher, but never followed the profession; having satisfied himself that he could not believe the doctrines of that or any other Church. For a few years he was a private tutor in various families in Scotland, among others that of the Marquis of Tweeddale; but ended by taking up his residence in London, and devoting himself to authorship. Nor had he any other means of support until 1819, when he obtained an appointment in the India House.

In this period of my father's life there are two things which it is impossible not to be struck with: one of them unfortunately a very common circumstance, the other a most uncommon one. The first is, that in his position, with no resource but the precarious one of writing in periodicals, he married and had a large family; conduct than which nothing could be more opposed, both as a matter of good sense and of duty, to the opinions which, at least at a later period of life, he strenuously upheld. The other circumstance is the extraordinary energy which was required to lead the life he led, with the disadvantages under which he laboured from the first, and with those which he brought upon himself by his marriage. It would have been no small thing, had he done no more than to support himself and his family during so many years by writing, without ever being in debt, or in any pecuniary difficulty; holding, as he did, opinions, both in politics and in religion, which were more odious to all persons of influence, and to the common run of prosperous Englishmen in that generation than either before or since; and being not only a man whom nothing would have induced to write against his convictions, but one who invariably threw into everything he wrote, as much of his convictions as he thought the circumstances would in any way permit: being, it must also be said, one who never did anything negligently; never undertook any task, literary or other, on which he did not conscientiously bestow all the labour necessary for performing it adequately. But he, with these burthens on him, planned, commenced, and completed, the History of India; and this in the course of about ten years, a shorter time than has been occupied (even by writers who had no other employment) in the production of almost any other historical work of equal bulk, and of anything approaching to the same amount of reading and research. And to this is to be added, that during the whole period, a considerable part of almost every day was employed in the instruction of his children: in the case of one of whom, myself, he exerted an amount of labour, care, and perseverance rarely, if ever, employed for a similar purpose, in endeavouring to give, according to his own conception, the highest order of intellectual education.

A man who, in his own practice, so vigorously acted up to the principle of losing no time, was likely to adhere to the same rule in the instruction of his pupil. I have no remembrance of the time when I began to learn Greek. I have been told that it was when I was three years old. My earliest recollection on the subject, is that of committing to memory what my father termed Vocables, being lists of common Greek words, with their signification in English, which he wrote out for me on cards. Of grammar, until

some years later, I learnt no more than the inflexions of
the nouns and verbs, but, after a course of vocables, proceeded at once to translation; and I faintly remember going
through Æsop's Fables, the first Greek book which I read.
The Anabasis, which I remember better, was the second.
I learnt no Latin until my eighth year. At that time I had
read, under my father's tuition, a number of Greek prose
authors, among whom I remember the whole of Herodotus,
and of Xenophon's Cyropædia and Memorials of Socrates;
some of the lives of the philosophers by Diogenes Laertius;
part of Lucian, and Isocrates' ad Demonicum and ad Nico-
clem. I also read, in 1813, the first six dialogues (in the
common arrangement) of Plato, from the Euthyphron
to the Theætetus inclusive: which last dialogue, I venture
to think, would have been better omitted, as it was totally
impossible I should understand it. But my father, in all
his teaching, demanded of me not only the utmost that I
could do, but much that I could by no possibility have done.
What he was himself willing to undergo for the sake of
my instruction, may be judged from the fact, that I went
through the whole process of preparing my Greek lessons
in the same room and at the same table at which he was
writing: and as in those days Greek and English lexicons
were not, and I could make no more use of a Greek and
Latin lexicon than could be made without having yet
begun to learn Latin, I was forced to have recourse to
him for the meaning of every word which I did not know.
This incessant interruption, he, one of the most impatient
of men, submitted to, and wrote under that interruption
several volumes of his History and all else that he had to
write during those years.

The only thing besides Greek, that I learnt as a lesson
in this part of my childhood, was arithmetic: this also my
father taught me: it was the task of the evenings, and I
well remember its disagreeableness. But the lessons were
only a part of the daily instruction I received. Much of it

consisted in the books I read by myself, and my father's discourses to me, chiefly during our walks. From 1810 to the end of 1813 we were living in Newington Green, then an almost rustic neighbourhood. My father's health required considerable and constant exercise, and he walked habitually before breakfast, generally in the green lanes towards Hornsey. In these walks I always accompanied him, and with my earliest recollections of green fields and wild flowers, is mingled that of the account I gave him daily of what I had read the day before. To the best of my remembrance, this was a voluntary rather than a prescribed exercise. I made notes on slips of paper while reading, and from these, in the morning walks, I told the story to him; for the books were chiefly histories, of which I read in this manner a great number: Robertson's histories, Hume, Gibbon; but my greatest delight, then and for long afterwards, was Watson's Philip the Second and Third. The heroic defence of the Knights of Malta against the Turks, and of the revolted provinces of the Netherlands against Spain, excited in me an intense and lasting interest. Next to Watson, my favourite historical reading was Hooke's History of Rome. Of Greece I had seen at that time no regular history, except school abridgments and the last two or three volumes of a translation of Rollin's Ancient History, beginning with Philip of Macedon. But I read with great delight Langhorne's translation of Plutarch. In English history, beyond the time at which Hume leaves off, I remember reading Burnet's History of his Own Time, though I cared little for anything in it except the wars and battles; and the historical part of the Annual Register, from the beginning to about 1788, when the volumes my father borrowed for me from Mr. Bentham left off. I felt a lively interest in Frederic of Prussia during his difficulties, and in Paoli, the Corsican patriot; but when I came to the American war, I took my part, like a child as I was (until set right by my father) on the wrong side, because it was called the

English side. In these frequent talks about the books I read, he used, as opportunity offered, to give me explanations and ideas respecting civilization, government, morality, mental cultivation, which he required me afterwards to restate to him in my own words. He also made me read, and give him a verbal account of, many books which would not have interested me sufficiently to induce me to read them of myself: among others, Millar's Historical View of the English Government, a book of great merit for its time, and which he highly valued; Mosheim's Ecclesiastical History, McCrie's Life of John Knox, and even Sewel's and Rutty's Histories of the Quakers. He was fond of putting into my hands books which exhibited men of energy and resource in unusual circumstances, struggling against difficulties and overcoming them: of such works I remember Beaver's African Memoranda, and Collins's account of the first settlement of New South Wales. Two books which I never wearied of reading were Anson's Voyage, so delightful to most young persons, and a Collection (Hawkesworth's, I believe) of Voyages round the World, in four volumes, beginning with Drake and ending with Cook and Bougainville. Of children's books, any more than of playthings, I had scarcely any, except an occasional gift from a relation or acquaintance: among those I had, Robinson Crusoe was preeminent, and continued to delight me through all my boyhood. It was no part however of my father's system to exclude books of amusement, though he allowed them very sparingly. Of such books he possessed at that time next to none, but he borrowed several for me; those which I remember are the Arabian Nights, Cazotte's Arabian Tales, Don Quixote, Miss Edgeworth's "Popular Tales," and a book of some reputation in its day, Brooke's Fool of Quality.

In my eighth year I commenced learning Latin, in conjunction with a younger sister, to whom I taught it as I went on, and who afterwards repeated the lessons to my father: and from this time, other sisters and brothers being successively added as pupils, a considerable part of my day's work consisted of this preparatory teaching. It was a part which I greatly disliked; the more so, as I was held responsible for the lessons of my pupils, in almost as full a sense as for my own: I however derived from this discipline the great advantage of learning more thoroughly and retaining more lastingly the things which I was set to teach: perhaps, too, the practice it afforded in explaining difficulties to others, may even at that age have been useful. In other respects, the experience of my boyhood is not favourable to the plan of teaching children by means of one another. The teaching, I am sure, is very inefficient as teaching, and I well knew that the relation between teacher and taught is not a good moral discipline to either. I went in this manner through the Latin grammar, and a considerable part of Cornelius Nepos and Cæsar's Commentaries, but afterwards added to the superintendence of these lessons, much longer ones of my own.

In the same year in which I began Latin, I made my first commencement in the Greek poets with the Iliad. After I had made some progress in this, my father put Pope's translation into my hands. It was the first English verse I had cared to read, and it became one of the books in which for many years I most delighted: I think I must have read it from twenty to thirty times through. I should not have thought it worth while to mention a taste apparently so natural to boyhood, if I had not, as I think, observed that the keen enjoyment of this brilliant specimen of narrative and versification is not so universal with boys, as I should have expected both *a priori* and from my individual experience. Soon after this time I commenced Euclid, and somewhat later, algebra, still under my father's tuition.

From my eighth to my twelfth year the Latin books which I remember reading were, the Bucolics of Virgil,

and the first six books of the Æneid; all Horace except
the Epodes; the Fables of Phædrus; the first five books
of Livy (to which from my love of the subject I voluntarily added, in my hours of leisure, the remainder of the
first decade); all Sallust; a considerable part of Ovid's
Metamorphoses; some plays of Terence; two or three
books of Lucretius; several of the Orations of Cicero, and
of his writings on oratory; also his letters to Atticus, my
father taking the trouble to translate to me from the
French the historical explanations in Mongault's notes. In
Greek I read the Iliad and Odyssey through; one or two
plays of Sophocles, Euripides, and Aristophanes, though
by these I profited little; all Thucydides; the Hellenics of
Xenophon; a great part of Demosthenes, Æschines, and
Lysias; Theocritus; Anacreon; part of the Anthology; a
little of Dionysius; several books of Polybius; and lastly
Aristotle's Rhetoric, which, as the first expressly scientific
treatise on any moral or psychological subject which I had
read, and containing many of the best observations of the
ancients on human nature and life, my father made me
study with peculiar care, and throw the matter of it into
synoptic tables. During the same years I learnt elementary geometry and algebra thoroughly, the differential cal-
culus and other portions of the higher mathematics far
from thoroughly: for my father, not having kept up this
part of his early acquired knowledge, could not spare time
to qualify himself for removing my difficulties, and left
me to deal with them, with little other aid than that of
books; while I was continually incurring his displeasure by
my inability to solve difficult problems for which he did
not see that I had not the necessary previous knowledge.

As to my private reading, I can only speak of what I
remember. History continued to be my strongest predi-
lection, and most of all ancient history. Mitford's Greece
I read continually; my father had put me on my guard
against the Tory prejudices of this writer, and his per-

versions of facts for the whitewashing of despots, and blackening of popular institutions. These points he discoursed on, exemplifying them from the Greek orators and historians, with such effect that in reading Mitford my sympathies were always on the contrary side to those of the author, and I could, to some extent, have argued the point against him: yet this did not diminish the ever new pleasure with which I read the book. Roman history, both in my old favourite, Hooke, and in Ferguson, continued to delight me. A book which, in spite of what is called the dryness of its style, I took great pleasure in, was the Ancient Universal History, through the incessant reading of which I had my head full of historical details concerning the obscurest ancient people, while about modern history, except detached passages, such as the Dutch war of independence, I knew and cared comparatively little. A voluntary exercise, to which throughout my boyhood I was much addicted, was what I called writing histories. I successively composed a Roman history, picked out of Hooke; an abridgment of the Ancient Universal History; a History of Holland, from my favourite Watson and from an anonymous compilation; and in my eleventh and twelfth year I occupied myself with writing what I flattered myself was something serious. This was no less than a history of the Roman Government, compiled (with the assistance of Hooke) from Livy and Dionysius: of which I wrote as much as would have made an octavo volume, extending to the epoch of the Licinian Laws. It was, in fact, an account of the struggles between the patricians and plebeians, which now engrossed all the interest in my mind which I had previously felt in the mere wars and conquests of the Romans. I discussed all the constitutional points as they arose: though quite ignorant of Niebuhr's researches, I, by such lights as my father had given me, vindicated the Agrarian Laws on the evidence of Livy, and upheld to the best of my ability the Roman democratic party. A few years later, in my contempt of my childish efforts, I destroyed all these papers, not then anticipating that I could ever feel any curiosity about my first attempts at writing and reasoning. My father encouraged me in this useful amusement, though, as I think judiciously, he never asked to see what I wrote; so that I did not feel that in writing it I was accountable to any one, nor had the chilling sensation of being under a critical eye.

But though these exercises in history were never a compulsory lesson, there was another kind of composition which was so, namely, writing verses, and it was one of the most disagreeable of my tasks. Greek and Latin verses I did not write, nor learnt the prosody of those languages. My father, thinking this not worth the time it required, contented himself with making me read aloud to him, and correcting false quantities. I never composed at all in Greek, even in prose, and but little in Latin. Not that my father could be indifferent to the value of this practice, in giving a thorough knowledge of those languages, but because there really was not time for it. The verses I was required to write were English. When I first read Pope's Homer, I ambitiously attempted to compose something of the same kind, and achieved as much as one book of a continuation of the Iliad. There, probably, the spontaneous promptings of my poetical ambition would have stopped; but the exercise, begun from choice, was continued by command. Conformably to my father's usual practice of explaining to me, as far as possible, the reasons for what he required me to do, he gave me, for this, as I well remember, two reasons highly characteristic of him: one was, that some things could be expressed better and more forcibly in verse than in prose: this, he said, was a real advantage. The other was, that people in general attached more value to verse than it deserved, and the power of writing it, was, on this account, worth acquiring. He generally left me to choose my own subjects, which, as far as I remember, were mostly addresses to some mythological personage or allegorical abstraction; but he made me translate into English verse many of Horace's shorter poems: I also remember his giving me Thomson's " Winter " to read, and afterwards making me attempt (without book) to write something myself on the same subject. The verses I wrote were, of course, the merest rubbish, nor did I ever attain any facility of versification, but the practice may have been useful in making it easier for me, at a later period, to acquire readiness of expression.[1] I had read, up to this time, very little English poetry, Shakespeare my father had put into my hands, chiefly for the sake of the historical plays, from which, however, I went on to the others. My father never was a great admirer of Shakespeare, the English idolatry of whom he used to attack with some severity. He cared little for any English poetry except Milton (for whom he had the highest admiration), Goldsmith, Burns, and Gray's Bard, which he preferred to his Elegy: perhaps I may add Cowper and Beattie. He had some value for Spenser, and I remember his reading to me (unlike his usual practice of making me read to him), the first book of the Fairie Queene; but I took little pleasure in it. The poetry of the present century he saw scarcely any merit in, and I hardly became acquainted with any of it till I was grown up to manhood, except the metrical romances of Walter Scott, which I read at his recommendation and was intensely delighted with; as I always was with animated narrative. Dryden's Poems were among my father's books, and many of these he made me read, but I never cared for any of them except

---

[1] In a subsequent stage of boyhood, when these exercises had ceased to be compulsory, like most youthful writers I wrote tragedies; under the inspiration not so much of Shakespeare as of Joanna Baillie, whose " Constantine Paleologus " in particular appeared to me one of the most glorious of human compositions. I still think it one of the best dramas of the last two centuries.

Alexander's Feast, which, as well as many of the songs in
Walter Scott, I used to sing internally, to a music of my
own: to some of the latter, indeed, I went so far as to
compose airs, which I still remember. Cowper's short
poems I read with some pleasure, but never got far into
the longer ones; and nothing in the two volumes interested
me like the prose account of his three hares. In my
thirteenth year I met with Campbell's Poems, among which
Lochiel, Hohenlinden, the Exile of Erin, and some others,
gave me sensations I had never before experienced from
poetry. Here, too, I made nothing of the longer poems,
except the striking opening of Gertrude of Wyoming, which
long kept its place in my feelings as the perfection of
pathos.

During this part of my childhood, one of my greatest
amusements was experimental science; in the theoretical,
however, not the practical sense of the word; not trying
experiments — a kind of discipline which I have often regretted not having had — nor even seeing, but merely
reading about them. I never remember being so wrapt
up in any book, as I was in Joyce's Scientific Dialogues;
and I was rather recalcitrant to my father's criticisms of the
bad reasoning respecting the first principles of physics,
which abounds in the early part of that work. I devoured
treatises on Chemistry, especially that of my father's early
friend and schoolfellow, Dr. Thomson, for years before I
attended a lecture or saw an experiment.

From about the age of twelve, I entered into another
and more advanced stage in my course of instruction; in
which the main object was no longer the aids and appliances
of thought, but the thoughts themselves. This commenced
with Logic, in which I began at once with the Organon,
and read it to the Analytics inclusive, but profited little by
the Posterior Analytics, which belong to a branch of speculation I was not yet ripe for. Contemporaneously with
the Organon, my father made me read the whole or parts

of several of the Latin treatises on the scholastic logic; giving each day to him, in our walks, a minute account of what I had read, and answering his numerous and searching questions. After this, I went in a similar manner, through the " Computatio sive Logica " of Hobbes, a work of a much higher order of thought than the books of the school logicians, and which he estimated very highly; in my own opinion beyond its merits, great as these are. It was his invariable practice, whatever studies he exacted from me, to make me as far as possible understand and feel the utility of them: and this he deemed peculiarly fitting in the case of the syllogistic logic, the usefulness of which had been impugned by so many writers of authority. I well remember how, and in what particular walk, in the neighbourhood of Bagshot Heath (where we were on a visit to his old friend Mr. Wallace, then one of the Mathematical Professors at Sandhurst) he first attempted by questions to make me think on the subject, and frame some conception of what constituted the utility of the syllogistic logic, and when I had failed in this, to make me understand it by explanations. The explanations did not make the matter at all clear to me at the time; but they were not therefore useless; they remained as a nucleus for my observations and reflections to crystallize upon; the import of his general remarks being interpreted to me, by the particular instances which came under my notice afterwards. My own consciousness and experience ultimately led me to appreciate quite as highly as he did, the value of an early practical familiarity with the school logic. I know nothing, in my education, to which I think myself more indebted for whatever capacity of thinking I have attained. The first intellectual operation in which I arrived at any proficiency, was dissecting a bad argument, and finding in what part the fallacy lay: and though whatever capacity of this sort I attained was due to the fact that it was an intellectual exercise in which I was most perseveringly drilled by my father, yet it is also

true that the school logic, and the mental habits acquired
in studying it, were among the principal instruments of this
drilling. I am persuaded that nothing, in modern education, tends so much, when properly used, to form exact
thinkers, who attach a precise meaning to words and propositions, and are not imposed on by vague, loose, or ambiguous
terms. The boasted influence of mathematical studies is
nothing to it; for in mathematical processes, none of the
real difficulties of correct ratiocination occur. It is also a
study peculiarly adapted to an early stage in the education
of philosophical students, since it does not presuppose the
slow process of acquiring, by experience and reflection,
valuable thoughts of their own. They may become capable
of disentangling the intricacies of confused and self-contra-
dictory thought, before their own thinking faculties are much
advanced; a power which, for want of some such discipline,
many otherwise able men altogether lack; and when they
have to answer opponents, only endeavour, by such arguments as they can command, to support the opposite conclusion, scarcely even attempting to confute the reasonings of
their antagonists; and, therefore, at the utmost, leaving the
question, as far as it depends on argument, a balanced one.

During this time, the Latin and Greek books which I continued to read with my father were chiefly such as were
worth studying, not for the language merely, but also for
the thoughts. This included much of the orators, and especially Demosthenes, some of whose principal orations I read
several times over, and wrote out, by way of exercise, a full
analysis of them. My father's comments on these orations
when I read them to him were very instructive to me. He
not only drew my attention to the insight they afforded
into Athenian institutions, and the principles of legislation
and government which they often illustrated, but pointed
out the skill and art of the orator — how everything important to his purpose was said at the exact moment when he
had brought the minds of his audience into the state most

fitted to receive it; how he made steal into their minds, gradually and by insinuation, thoughts which, if expressed in a
more direct manner would have aroused their opposition.
Most of these reflections were beyond my capacity of full
comprehension at the time; but they left seed behind, which
germinated in due season. At this time I also read the whole
of Tacitus, Juvenal, and Quintilian. The latter, owing to
his obscure style and to the scholastic details of which many
parts of his treatise are made up, is little read, and seldom
sufficiently appreciated. His book is a kind of encyclopædia
of the thoughts of the ancients on the whole field of education and culture; and I have retained through life many
valuable ideas which I can distinctly trace to my reading of
him, even at that early age. It was at this period that I
read, for the first time, some of the most important dialogues
of Plato, in particular the Gorgias, the Protagoras, and the
Republic. There is no author to whom my father thought
himself more indebted for his own mental culture, than
Plato, or whom he more frequently recommended to young
students. I can bear similar testimony in regard to myself.
The Socratic method, of which the Platonic dialogues are
the chief example, is unsurpassed as a discipline for correcting the errors, and clearing up the confusions incident to the
intellectus sibi permissus, the understanding which has made
up all its bundles of associations under the guidance of
popular phraseology. The close, searching *elenchus* by
which the man of vague generalities is constrained either
to express his meaning to himself in definite terms, or to
confess that he does not know what he is talking about; the
perpetual testing of all general statements by particular instances; the siege in form which is laid to the meaning of
large abstract terms, by fixing upon some still larger class-
name which includes that and more, and dividing down to
the thing sought — marking out its limits and definition
by a series of accurately drawn distinctions between it and
each of the cognate objects which are successively parted off

from it — all this, as an education for precise thinking, is inestimable, and all this, even at that age, took such hold of me that it became part of my own mind. I have felt ever since that the title of Platonist belongs by far better right to those who have been nourished in, and have endeavoured to practise Plato's mode of investigation, than to those who are distinguished only by the adoption of certain dogmatical conclusions, drawn mostly from the least intelligible of his works, and which the character of his mind and writings makes it uncertain whether he himself regarded as anything more than poetic fancies, or philosophic conjectures.

In going through Plato and Demosthenes, since I could now read these authors, as far as the language was concerned, with perfect ease, I was not required to construe them sentence by sentence, but to read them aloud to my father, answering questions when asked: but the particular attention which he paid to elocution (in which his own excellence was remarkable) made this reading aloud to him a most painful task. Of all things which he required me to do, there was none which I did so constantly ill, or in which he so perpetually lost his temper with me. He had thought much on the principles of the art of reading, especially the most neglected part of it, the inflections of the voice, or *modulation* as writers on elocution call it (in contrast with *articulation* on the one side, and *expression* on the other), and had reduced it to rules, grounded on the logical analysis of a sentence. These rules he strongly impressed upon me, and took me severely to task for every violation of them: but I even then remarked (though I did not venture to make the remark to him) that though he reproached me when I read a sentence ill, and *told* me how I ought to have read it, he never, by reading it himself, *showed* me how it ought to be read. A defect running through his otherwise admirable modes of instruction, as it did through all his modes of thought, was that of trusting too much to the intelligibleness of the abstract, when not embodied in the concrete. It was

at a much later period of my youth, when practising elocution by myself, or with companions of my own age, that I
for the first time understood the object of his rules, and saw
the psychological grounds of them. At that time I and
others followed out the subject into its ramifications and
could have composed a very useful treatise, grounded on
my father's principles. He himself left those principles
and rules unwritten. I regret that when my mind was full
of the subject, from systematic practice, I did not put them,
and our improvements of them, into a formal shape.

A book which contributed largely to my education, in the
best sense of the term, was my father's History of India.
It was published in the beginning of 1818. During the
year previous, while it was passing through the press, I used
to read the proof sheets to him; or rather, I read the manuscript to him while he corrected the proofs. The number
of new ideas which I received from this remarkable book,
and the impulse and stimulus as well as guidance given to
my thoughts by its criticisms and disquisitions on society
and civilization in the Hindoo part, on institutions and the
acts of governments in the English part, made my early
familarity with it eminently useful to my subsequent progress. And though I can perceive deficiencies in it now as
compared with a perfect standard, I still think it, if not
the most, one of the most instructive histories ever written,
and one of the books from which most benefit may be derived by a mind in the course of making up its opinions.

The Preface, among the most characteristic of my father's
writings, as well as the richest in materials of thought, gives
a picture which may be entirely depended on, of the sentiments and expectations with which he wrote the History.
Saturated as the book is with the opinions and modes of
judgment of a democratic radicalism then regarded as extreme; and treating with a severity, at that time most unusual, the English Constitution, the English law, and all
parties and classes who possessed any considerable influence

in the country; he may have expected reputation, but certainly not advancement in life, from its publication; nor could he have supposed that it would raise up anything but enemies for him in powerful quarters: least of all could he have expected favour from the East India Company, to whose commercial privileges he was unqualifiedly hostile, and on the acts of whose government he had made so many severe comments: though, in various parts of his book, he bore a testimony in their favour, which he felt to be their just due, namely, that no government had on the whole given so much proof, to the extent of its lights, of good intention towards its subjects; and that if the acts of any other government had the light of publicity as completely let in upon them, they would, in all probability, still less bear scrutiny.

On learning, however, in the spring of 1819, about a year after the publication of the History, that the East India Directors desired to strengthen the part of their home establishment which was employed in carrying on the correspondence with India, my father declared himself a candidate for that employment, and, to the credit of the Directors, successfully. He was appointed one of the Assistants of the Examiner of India Correspondence; officers whose duty it was to prepare drafts of despatches to India, for consideration by the Directors, in the principal departments of administration. In this office, and in that of Examiner, which he subsequently attained, the influence which his talents, his reputation, and his decision of character gave him, with superiors who really desired the good government of India, enabled him to a great extent to throw into his drafts of despatches, and to carry through the ordeal of the Court of Directors and Board of Control, without having their force much weakened, his real opinions on Indian subjects. In his History he had set forth, for the first time, many of the true principles of Indian administration: and his despatches, following his History, did more than had ever been done before to promote the improvement of India, and teach Indian officials to understand their business. If a selection of them were published, they would, I am convinced, place his character as a practical statesman fully on a level with his eminence as a speculative writer.

This new employment of his time caused no relaxation in his attention to my education. It was in this same year, 1819, that he took me through a complete course of political economy. His loved and intimate friend, Ricardo, had shortly before published the book which formed so great an epoch in political economy; a book which never would have been published or written, but for the entreaty and strong encouragement of my father; for Ricardo, the most modest of men, though firmly convinced of the truth of his doctrines, deemed himself so little capable of doing them justice in exposition and expression, that he shrank from the idea of publicity. The same friendly encouragement induced Ricardo, a year or two later, to become a member of the House of Commons; where, during the few remaining years of his life, unhappily cut short in the full vigour of his intellect, he rendered so much service to his and my father's opinions both on political economy and on other subjects.

Though Ricardo's great work was already in print, no didactic treatise embodying its doctrines, in a manner fit for learners, had yet appeared. My father, therefore, commenced instructing me in the science by a sort of lectures, which he delivered to me in our walks. He expounded each day a portion of the subject, and I gave him next day a written account of it, which he made me rewrite over and over again until it was clear, precise, and tolerably complete. In this manner I went through the whole extent of the science; and the written outline of it which resulted from my daily *compte rendu*, served him afterwards as notes from which to write his Elements of Political Economy. After this I read Ricardo, giving an account daily of what I read, and discussing, in the best manner I could, the collateral points which offered themselves in our progress.

On Money, as the most intricate part of the subject, he made me read in the same manner Ricardo's admirable pamphlets, written during what was called the Bullion controversy; to these succeeded Adam Smith; and in this reading it was one of my father's main objects to make me apply to Smith's more superficial view of political economy, the superior lights of Ricardo, and detect what was fallacious in Smith's arguments, or erroneous in any of his conclusions. Such a mode of instruction was excellently calculated to form a thinker; but it required to be worked by a thinker, as close and vigorous as my father. The path was a thorny one, even to him, and I am sure it was so to me, notwithstanding the strong interest I took in the subject. He was often, and much beyond reason, provoked by my failures in cases where success could not have been expected; but in the main his method was right, and it succeeded. I do not believe that any scientific teaching ever was more thorough, or better fitted for training the faculties, than the mode in which logic and political economy were taught to me by my father. Striving, even in an exaggerated degree, to call forth the activity of my faculties, by making me find out everything for myself, he gave his explanations not before, but after, I had felt the full force of the difficulties; and not only gave me an accurate knowledge of these two great subjects, as far as they were then understood, but made me a thinker on both. I thought for myself almost from the first, and occasionally thought differently from him, though for a long time only on minor points, and making his opinion the ultimate standard. At a later period I even occasionally convinced him, and altered his opinion on some points of detail: which I state to his honour, not my own. It at once exemplifies his perfect candour, and the real worth of his method of teaching.

At this point concluded what can properly be called my

lessons: when I was about fourteen I left England for more than a year; and after my return, though my studies went on under my father's general direction, he was no longer my schoolmaster. I shall therefore pause here, and turn back to matters of a more general nature connected with the part of my life and education included in the preceding reminiscences.

In the course of instruction which I have partially retraced, the point most superficially apparent is the great effort to give, during the years of childhood an amount of knowledge in what are considered the higher branches of education, which is seldom acquired (if acquired at all) until the age of manhood. The result of the experiment shows the ease with which this may be done, and places in a strong light the wretched waste of so many precious years as are spent in acquiring the modicum of Latin and Greek commonly taught to schoolboys; a waste, which has led so many educational reformers to entertain the ill-judged proposal of discarding these languages altogether from general education. If I had been by nature extremely quick of apprehension, or had possessed a very accurate and retentive memory, or were of a remarkably active and energetic character, the trial would not be conclusive; but in all these natural gifts I am rather below than above par; what I could do, could assuredly be done by any boy or girl of average capacity and healthy physical constitution: and if I have accomplished anything, I owe it, among other fortunate circumstances, to the fact that through the early training bestowed on me by my father, I started, I may fairly say, with an advantage of a quarter of a century over my contemporaries.

There was one cardinal point in this training, of which I have already given some indication, and which, more than anything else, was the cause of whatever good it effected. Most boys or youths who have had much knowledge drilled into them, have their mental capacities not strengthened, but overlaid by it. They are crammed with mere facts, and with the opinions or phrases of other people, and these are accepted as a substitute for the power to form opinions of their own: and thus the sons of eminent fathers, who have spared no pains in their education, so often grow up mere parroters of what they have learnt, incapable of using their minds except in the furrows traced for them. Mine, however, was not an education of cram. My father never permitted anything which I learnt to degenerate into a mere exercise of memory. He strove to make the understanding not only go along with every step of the teaching, but, if possible, precede it. Anything which could be found out by thinking I never was told, until I had exhausted my efforts to find it out for myself. As far as I can trust my remembrance, I acquitted myself very lamely in this department; my recollection of such matters is almost wholly of failures, hardly ever of success. It is true the failures were often in things in which success in so early a stage of my progress, was almost impossible. I remember at some time in my thirteenth year, on my happening to use the word idea, he asked me what an idea was; and expressed some displeasure at my ineffectual efforts to define the word: I recollect also his indignation at my using the common expression that something was true in theory but required correction in practice; and how, after making me vainly strive to define the word theory, he explained its meaning, and showed the fallacy of the vulgar form of speech which I had used; leaving me fully persuaded that in being unable to give a correct definition of Theory, and in speaking of it as something which might be at variance with practice, I had shown unparalleled ignorance. In this he seems, and perhaps was, very unreasonable; but I think, only in being angry at my failure. A pupil from whom nothing is ever demanded which he cannot do, never does all he can.

One of the evils most liable to attend on any sort of early proficiency, and which often fatally blights its promise, my father most anxiously guarded against. This was self-conceit. He kept me, with extreme vigilance, out of the way of hearing myself praised, or of being led to make self-flattering comparisons between myself and others. From his own intercourse with me I could derive none but a very humble opinion of myself; and the standard of comparison he always held up to me, was not what other people did, but what a man could and ought to do. He completely succeeded in preserving me from the sort of influences he so much dreaded. I was not at all aware that my attainments were anything unusual at my age. If I accidentally had my attention drawn to the fact that some other boy knew less than myself — which happened less often than might be imagined — I concluded, not that I knew much, but that he, for some reason or other, knew little, or that his knowledge was of a different kind from mine. My state of mind was not humility, but neither was it arrogance. I never thought of saying to myself, I am, or I can do, so and so. I neither estimated myself highly nor lowly: I did not estimate myself at all. If I thought anything about myself, it was that I was rather backward in my studies, since I always found myself so, in comparison with what my father expected from me. I assert this with confidence, though it was not the impression of various persons who saw me in my childhood. They, as I have since found, thought me greatly and disagreeably self-conceited; probably because I was disputatious, and did not scruple to give direct contradictions to things which I heard said. I suppose I acquired this bad habit from having been encouraged in an unusual degree to talk on matters beyond my age, and with grown persons, while I never had inculcated in me the usual respect for them. My father did not correct this ill-breeding and impertinence, probably from not being aware of it, for I was always too much in awe of him to be otherwise than extremely subdued and quiet in his presence. Yet with all this I had no notion of any superiority in myself; and well was it for me that I had not. I remember the very place in Hyde Park where, in my fourteenth year, on the eve of leaving my father's house for a long absence, he told me that I should find, as I got acquainted with new people, that I had been taught many things which youths of my age did not commonly know; and that many persons would be disposed to talk to me of this, and to compliment me upon it. What other things he said on this topic I remember very imperfectly; but he wound up by saying, that whatever I knew more than others, could not be ascribed to any merit in me, but to the very unusual advantage which had fallen to my lot, of having a father who was able to teach me, and willing to give the necessary trouble and time; that it was no matter of praise to me, if I knew more than those who had not had a similar advantage, but the deepest disgrace to me if I did not. I have a distinct remembrance, that the suggestion thus for the first time made to me, that I knew more than other youths who were considered well educated, was to me a piece of information, to which, as to all other things which my father told me, I gave implicit credence, but which did not at all impress me as a personal matter. I felt no disposition to glorify myself upon the circumstance that there were other persons who did not know what I knew; nor had I ever flattered myself that my acquirements, whatever they might be, were any merit of mine: but, now when my attention was called to the subject, I felt that what my father had said respecting my peculiar advantages was exactly the truth and common sense of the matter, and it fixed my opinion and feeling from that time forward.

It is evident that this, among many other of the purposes of my father's scheme of education, could not have been accomplished if he had not carefully kept me from having any great amount of intercourse with other boys. He was earnestly bent upon my escaping not only the ordinary corrupting influence which boys exercise over boys, but the contagion of vulgar modes of thought and feeling; and for this he was willing that I should pay the price of inferiority in the accomplishments which schoolboys in all countries chiefly cultivate. The deficiencies in my education were principally in the things which boys learn from being turned out to shift for themselves, and from being brought together in large numbers. From temperance and much walking, I grew up healthy and hardy, though not muscular; but I could do no feats of skill or physical strength, and knew none of the ordinary bodily exercises. It was not that play, or time for it, was refused me. Though no holidays were allowed, lest the habit of work should be broken, and a taste for idleness acquired, I had ample leisure in every day to amuse myself; but as I had no boy companions, and the animal need of physical activity was satisfied by walking, my amusements, which were mostly solitary, were in general of a quiet, if not a bookish turn, and gave little stimulus to any other kind even of mental activity than that which was already called forth by my studies: I consequently remained long, and in a less degree have always remained, inexpert in anything requiring manual dexterity; my mind as well as my hands, did its work very lamely when it was applied, or ought to have been applied, to the practical details which, as they are the chief interest of life to the majority of men, are also the things in which whatever mental capacity they have, chiefly shows itself: I was constantly meriting reproof by inattention, inobservance, and general slackness of mind in matters of daily life. My father was the extreme opposite in these particulars: his senses and mental faculties were always on the alert; he carried decision and energy of character in his whole manner and into every action of life: and this, as much as his talents, contributed to the strong impression which he always made upon those with whom he came into personal contact. But the children of energetic parents, frequently grow up un-energetic, because they lean on their parents, and the parents are energetic for them. The education which my father gave me, was in itself much more fitted for training me to *know* than to *do*. Not that he was unaware of my deficiencies; both as a boy and as a youth I was incessantly smarting under his severe admonitions on the subject. There was anything but insensibility or tolerance on his part towards such shortcomings: but, while he saved me from the demoralizing effects of school life, he made no effort to provide me with any sufficient substitute for its practicalizing influences. Whatever qualities he himself, probably, had acquired without difficulty or special training, he seems to have supposed that I ought to acquire as easily. He had not, I think, bestowed the same amount of thought and attention on this, as on most other branches of education; and here, as well as in some other points of my tuition, he seems to have expected effects without causes.

CHAPTER II

MORAL INFLUENCES IN EARLY YOUTH. MY
FATHER'S CHARACTER AND OPINIONS.

IN my education, as in that of everyone, the moral influences, which are so much more important than all others,
are also the most complicated, and the most difficult to
specify with any approach to completeness. Without
attempting the hopeless task of detailing the circumstances
by which, in this respect, my early character may have been
shaped, I shall confine myself to a few leading points, which
form an indispensable part of any true account of my education.

I was brought up from the first without any religious
belief, in the ordinary acceptation of the term. My father,
educated in the creed of Scotch presbyterianism, had
by his own studies and reflections been early led to reject
not only the belief in revelation, but the foundations of
what is commonly called Natural Religion. I have heard
him say, that the turning point of his mind on the subject
was reading Butler's Analogy. That work, of which he
always continued to speak with respect, kept him, as he said,
for some considerable time, a believer in the divine authority of Christianity; by proving to him, that whatever are
the difficulties in believing that the Old and New Testa-
ments proceed from, or record the acts of, a perfectly wise
and good being, the same and still greater difficulties stand
in the way of the belief, that a being of such a character
can have been the Maker of the universe. He considered
Butler's argument as conclusive against the only opponents
for whom it was intended. Those who admit an omnipotent
as well as perfectly just and benevolent maker and ruler

of such a world as this, can say little against Christianity but
what can, with at least equal force, be retorted against themselves. Finding, therefore, no halting place in Deism, he
remained in a state of perplexity, until, doubtless after
many struggles, he yielded to the conviction, that, concerning
the origin of things nothing whatever can be known. This
is the only correct statement of his opinion; for dogmatic
atheism he looked upon as absurd; as most of those, whom
the world has considered Atheists, have always done.
These particulars are important, because they show that my
father's rejection of all that is called religious belief, was
not, as many might suppose, primarily a matter of logic and
evidence: the grounds of it were moral, still more than
intellectual. He found it impossible to believe that a world
so full of evil was the work of an Author combining infinite
power with perfect goodness and righteousness. His intellect spurned the subtleties by which men attempt to blind
themselves to this open contradiction. The Sabæan, or
Manichæan theory of a Good and Evil Principle, struggling
against each other for the government of the universe, he
would not have equally condemned; and I have heard him
express surprise, that no one revived it in our time. He
would have regarded it as a mere hypothesis; but he would
have ascribed to it no depraving influence. As it was, his
aversion to religion, in the sense usually attached to the
term, was of the same kind with that of Lucretius: he
regarded it with the feelings due not to a mere mental
delusion, but to a great moral evil. He looked upon it as
the greatest enemy of morality: first, by setting up factitious
excellencies, — belief in creeds, devotional feelings, and
ceremonies, not connected with the good of human kind, —
and causing these to be accepted as substitutes for genuine
virtues: but above all, by radically vitiating the standard of
morals; making it consist in doing the will of a being, on
whom it lavishes indeed all the phrases of adulation, but
whom in sober truth it depicts as eminently hateful. I have

a hundred times heard him say, that all ages and nations have represented their gods as wicked, in a constantly increasing progression, that mankind have gone on adding trait after trait till they reached the most perfect conception of wickedness which the human mind can devise, and have called this God, and prostrated themselves before it. This *ne plus ultra* of wickedness he considered to be embodied in what is commonly presented to mankind as the creed of Christianity. Think (he used to say) of a being who would make a Hell — who would create the human race with the infallible foreknowledge, and therefore with the intention, that the great majority of them were to be consigned to horrible and everlasting torment. The time, I believe, is drawing near when this dreadful conception of an object of worship will be no longer identified with Christianity; and when all persons, with any sense of moral good and evil, will look upon it with the same indignation with which my father regarded it. My father was as well aware as anyone that Christians do not, in general, undergo the demoralizing consequences which seem inherent in such a creed, in the manner or to the extent which might have been expected from it. The same slovenliness of thought, and subjection of the reason to fears, wishes, and affections, which enable them to accept a theory involving a contradiction in terms, prevents them from perceiving the logical consequences of the theory. Such is the facility with which mankind believe at one and the same time things inconsistent with one another, and so few are those who draw from what they receive as truths, any consequences but those recommended to them by their feelings, that multitudes have held the undoubting belief in an Omnipotent Author of Hell, and have nevertheless identified that being with the best conception they were able to form of perfect goodness. Their worship was not paid to the demon which such a being as they imagined would really be, but to their own idea of excellence. The evil is, that such a belief keeps the ideal wretchedly low; and opposes the most obstinate resistance to all thought which has a tendency to raise it higher. Believers shrink from every train of ideas which would lead the mind to a clear conception and an elevated standard of excellence, because they feel (even when they do not distinctly see) that such a standard would conflict with many of the dispensations of nature, and with much of what they are accustomed to consider as the Christian creed. And thus morality continues a matter of blind tradition, with no consistent principle, nor even any consistent feeling, to guide it.

It would have been wholly inconsistent with my father's ideas of duty, to allow me to acquire impressions contrary to his convictions and feelings respecting religion: and he impressed upon me from the first, that the manner in which the world came into existence was a subject on which nothing was known: that the question, "Who made me?" cannot be answered, because we have no experience or authentic information from which to answer it; and that any answer only throws the difficulty a step further back, since the question immediately presents itself, Who made God? He, at the same time, took care that I should be acquainted with what had been thought by mankind on these impenetrable problems. I have mentioned at how early an age he made me a reader of ecclesiastical history; and he taught me to take the strongest interest in the Reformation, as the great and decisive contest against priestly tyranny for liberty of thought.

I am thus one of the very few examples, in this country, of one who has, not thrown off religious belief, but never had it: I grew up in a negative state with regard to it. I looked upon the modern exactly as I did upon the ancient religion, as something which in no way concerned me. It did not seem to me more strange that English people should believe what I did not, than that the men I read of in Herodotus should have done so. History had made the variety of opinions among mankind a fact familiar to me, and this was but a prolongation of that fact. This point in my early education had, however, incidentally one bad consequence deserving notice. In giving me an opinion contrary to that of the world, my father thought it necessary to give it as one which could not prudently be avowed to the world. This lesson of keeping my thoughts to myself, at that early age, was attended with some moral disadvantages; though my limited intercourse with strangers, especially such as were likely to speak to me on religion, prevented me from being placed in the alternative of avowal or hypocrisy. I remember two occasions in my boyhood, on which I felt myself in this alternative, and in both cases I avowed my disbelief and defended it. My opponents were boys, considerably older than myself: one of them I certainly staggered at the time, but the subject was never renewed between us: the other who was surprised, and somewhat shocked, did his best to convince me for some time, without effect.

The great advance in liberty of discussion, which is one of the most important differences between the present time and that of my childhood, has greatly altered the moralities of this question; and I think that few men of my father's intellect and public spirit, holding with such intensity of moral conviction as he did, unpopular opinions on religion, or on any other of the great subjects of thought, would now either practise or inculcate the withholding of them from the world, unless in the cases, becoming fewer every day, in which frankness on these subjects would either risk the loss of means of subsistence, or would amount to exclusion from some sphere of usefulness peculiarly suitable to the capacities of the individual. On religion in particular the time appears to me to have come, when it is the duty of all who being qualified in point of knowledge, have on mature consideration satisfied themselves that the current opinions are not only false but hurtful, to make their dissent known; at least, if they are among those whose station or reputation, gives their opinion a chance of being attended to. Such an avowal would put an end, at once and for ever, to the vulgar prejudice, that what is called, very improperly, unbelief, is connected with any bad qualities either of mind or heart. The world would be astonished if it knew how great a proportion of its brightest ornaments — of those most distinguished even in popular estimation for wisdom and virtue — are complete sceptics in religion; many of them refraining from avowal, less from personal considerations, than from a conscientious, though now in my opinion a most mistaken apprehension, lest by speaking out what would tend to weaken existing beliefs, and by consequence (as they suppose) existing restraints, they should do harm instead of good.

Of unbelievers (so called) as well as of believers, there are many species, including almost every variety of moral type. But the best among them, as no one who has had opportunities of really knowing them will hesitate to affirm (believers rarely have that opportunity), are more genuinely religious, in the best sense of the word religion, than those who exclusively arrogate to themselves the title. The liberality of the age, or in other words the weakening of the obstinate prejudice which makes men unable to see what is before their eyes because it is contrary to their expectations, has caused it to be very commonly admitted that a Deist may be truly religious: but if religion stands for any graces of character and not for mere dogma, the assertion may equally be made of many whose belief is far short of Deism. Though they may think the proof incomplete that the universe is a work of design, and though they assuredly disbelieve that it can have an Author and Governor who is absolute in power as well as perfect in goodness, they have that which constitutes the principal worth of all religions whatever, an ideal conception of a Perfect Being, to which they habitually refer as the guide of their conscience; and this ideal of Good is usually far nearer to perfection than the objective Deity of those, who think themselves obliged to find absolute goodness in the author of a world so crowded with suffering and so deformed by injustice as ours.

My father's moral convictions, wholly dissevered from religion, were very much of the character of those of the Greek philosophers; and were delivered with the force and decision which characterized all that came from him. Even at the very early age at which I read with him the Memorabilia of Xenophon, I imbibed from that work and from his comments a deep respect for the character of Socrates; who stood in my mind as a model of ideal excellence: and I well remember how my father at that time impressed upon me the lesson of the " Choice of Hercules." At a somewhat later period the lofty moral standard exhibited in the writings of Plato operated upon me with great force. My father's moral inculcations were at all times mainly those of the " Socratici viri;" justice, temperance (to which he gave a very extended application), veracity, perseverance, readiness to encounter pain and especially labour; regard for the public good; estimation of persons according to their merits, and of things according to their intrinsic usefulness; a life of exertion in contradiction to one of self-indulgent sloth. These and other moralities he conveyed in brief sentences, uttered as occasion arose, of grave exhortation, or stern reprobation and contempt.

But though direct moral teaching does much, indirect does more; and the effect my father produced on my character, did not depend solely on what he said or did with that direct object, but also, and still more, on what manner of man he was.

In his views of life he partook of the character of the Stoic, the Epicurean, and the Cynic, not in the modern but the ancient sense of the word. In his personal qualities the Stoic predominated. His standard of morals was Epicurean, inasmuch as it was utilitarian, taking as the exclusive test of right and wrong, the tendency of actions to produce pleasure or pain. But he had (and this was the Cynic element) scarcely any belief in pleasure; at least in his later years, of which alone, on this point, I can speak confidently. He was not insensible to pleasures; but he deemed very few of them worth the price which, at least in the present state of society, must be paid for them. The greater number of miscarriages in life, he considered to be attributable to the overvaluing of pleasures. Accordingly, temperance, in the large sense intended by the Greek philosophers — stopping short at the point of moderation in all indulgences — was with him, as with them, almost the central point of educational precept. His inculcations of this virtue fill a large place in my childish remembrances. He thought human life a poor thing at best, after the freshness of youth and of unsatisfied curiosity had gone by. This was a topic on which he did not often speak, especially, it may be supposed, in the presence of young persons: but when he did, it was with an air of settled and profound conviction. He would sometimes say, that if life were made what it might be, by good government and good education, it would be worth having: but he never spoke with anything like enthusiasm even of that possibility. He never varied in rating intellectual enjoyments above all others, even in value as pleasures, independently of their ulterior benefits. The pleasures of the benevolent affections he placed high in the scale; and used to say, that he had never known a happy old man, except those who were able to live over again in the pleasures of the young. For passionate emotions of all sorts, and for everything which has been said or written in exaltation of them, he professed the greatest contempt. He regarded them as a form of madness. "The intense" was with him a bye-word of scornful disapprobation. He regarded as an aberration of the moral standard of modern times, compared with that of the ancients, the great stress laid upon feeling. Feelings, as such, he considered to be no proper subjects of praise or blame. Right and wrong, good and bad, he regarded as qualities solely of conduct — of acts and omissions; there being no feeling which may not lead, and does not frequently lead, either to good or to bad actions: conscience itself, the very desire to act right, often leading people to act wrong. Consistently carrying out the doctrine, that the object of praise and blame should be the discouragement of wrong conduct and the encouragement of right, he refused to let his praise or blame be influenced by the motive of the agent. He blamed as severely what he thought a bad action, when the motive was a feeling of duty, as if the agents had been consciously evil doers. He would not have accepted as a plea in mitigation for inquisitors, that they sincerely believed burning heretics to be an obligation of conscience. But though he did not allow honesty of purpose to soften his disapprobation of actions, it had its full effect on his estimation of characters. No one prized conscientiousness and rectitude of intention more highly, or was more incapable of valuing any person in whom he did not feel assurance of it. But he disliked people quite as much for any other deficiency, provided he thought it equally likely to make them act ill. He disliked, for instance, a fanatic in any bad cause, as much or more than one who adopted the same cause from self-interest, because he thought him even more likely to be practically mischievous. And thus, his aversion to many intellectual errors, or what he regarded as such, partook, in a certain sense, of the character of a moral feeling. All this is merely saying that he, in a degree once common, but now very unusual, threw his feelings into his opinions; which truly it is difficult to understand how any one who possesses much of both, can fail to do. None but those who do not care about opinions, will confound it with intolerance. Those, who having opinions which they hold to be immensely important, and their contraries to be prodigiously hurtful, have any deep regard for the general good, will necessarily dislike, as a class and in the abstract, those who think wrong what they think right, and right what they think wrong: though they need not therefore be, nor was my father, insensible to good qualities in an opponent, nor governed in their estimation of individuals by one general presumption, instead of by the whole of their character. I grant that an earnest person, being no more infallible than other men, is liable to dislike people on account of opinions which do not merit dislike; but if he neither himself does them any ill office, nor connives at its being done by others, he is not intolerant: and the forbearance which flows from a conscientious sense of the importance to mankind of the equal freedom of all opinions, is the only tolerance which is commendable, or, to the highest moral order of minds, possible.

It will be admitted, that a man of the opinions, and the character, above described, was likely to leave a strong moral impression on any mind principally formed by him, and that his moral teaching was not likely to err on the side of laxity or indulgence. The element which was chiefly deficient in his moral relation to his children was that of tenderness. I do not believe that this deficiency lay in his own nature. I believe him to have had much more feeling than he habitually showed, and much greater capacities of feeling than were ever developed. He resembled most Englishmen in being ashamed of the signs of feeling, and by the absence of demonstration, starving the feelings themselves. If we consider further that he was in the trying position of sole teacher, and add to this that his temper was constitutionally irritable, it is impossible not to feel true pity for a father who did, and strove to do, so much for his children, who would have so valued their affection, yet who must have been constantly feeling that fear of him was drying it up at its source. This was no longer the case later in life, and with his younger children. They loved him tenderly: and if I cannot say so much of myself, I was always loyally devoted to him. As regards my own education, I hesitate to pronounce whether I was more a loser or gainer by his severity. It was not such as to prevent me from having a happy childhood. And I do not believe that boys can be induced to apply themselves with vigour, and what is so much more difficult, persever-ance, to dry and irksome studies, by the sole force of persuasion and soft words. Much must be done, and much must be learnt, by children, for which rigid discipline, and known liability to punishment, are indispensable as means. It is, no doubt, a very laudable effort, in modern teaching, to render as much as possible of what the young are re-quired to learn, easy and interesting to them. But when this principle is pushed to the length of not requiring them to learn anything *but* what has been made easy and interest-ing, one of the chief objects of education is sacrificed. I rejoice in the decline of the old brutal and tyrannical system of teaching, which, however, did succeed in en-forcing habits of application; but the new, as it seems to me, is training up a race of men who will be incapable of doing anything which is disagreeable to them. I do not, then, believe that fear, as an element in education, can be dispensed with; but I am sure that it ought not to be the main element; and when it predominates so much as to preclude love and confidence on the part of the child to those who should be the unreservedly trusted advisers of after years, and perhaps to seal up the fountains of frank and spontaneous communicativeness in the child's nature, it is an evil for which a large abatement must be made from the benefits, moral and intellectual, which may flow from any other part of the education.

During this first period of my life, the habitual fre-quenters of my father's house were limited to a very few persons, most of them little known to the world, but whom personal worth, and more or less of congeniality with at least his political opinions (not so frequently to be met with then as since) inclined him to cultivate; and his conversations with them I listened to with interest and instruction. My being an habitual inmate of my father's study made me acquainted with the dearest of his friends, David Ricardo, who by his benevolent countenance, and kindliness of manner, was very attractive to young persons, and who after I became a student of political economy, invited me to his house and to walk with him in order to converse on the subject. I was a more frequent visitor (from about 1817 or 1818) to Mr. Hume, who, born in the same part of Scotland as my father, and having been, I rather think, a younger schoolfellow or college companion of his, had on returning from India renewed their youthful acquaintance, and who coming like many others greatly under the influence of my father's intellect and energy of character, was induced partly by that influence to go into Parliament, and there adopt the line of conduct which has given him an honourable place in the history of his country. Of Mr. Bentham I saw much more, owing to the close intimacy which existed between him and my father. I do not know how soon after my father's first arrival in England they became acquainted. But my father was the earliest Englishman of any great mark, who thoroughly understood, and in the main adopted, Bentham's general views of ethics, government and law: and this was a natural foundation for sympathy between them, and made them familiar companions in a period of Bentham's life during which he admitted much fewer visitors than was the case subsequently. At this time Mr. Bentham passed some part of every year at Barrow Green House, in a beautiful part of the Surrey hills, a few miles from Godstone, and there I each summer accompanied my father in a long visit. In 1813 Mr. Bentham, my father, and I made an excursion, which included Oxford, Bath and Bristol, Exeter, Plymouth, and Portsmouth. In this journey I saw many things which were instructive to me, and acquired my first taste for

natural scenery, in the elementary form of fondness for a
"view." In the succeeding winter we moved into a house
very near Mr. Bentham's, which my father rented from
him, in Queen Square, Westminster. From 1814 to 1817
Mr. Bentham lived during half of each year at Ford Abbey,
in Somersetshire (or rather in a part of Devonshire surrounded by Somersetshire), which intervals I had the
advantage of passing at that place. This sojourn was, I
think, an important circumstance in my education. Nothing contributes more to nourish elevation of sentiments in
a people, than the large and free character of their habita-
tions. The middle-age architecture, the baronial hall, and
the spacious and lofty rooms, of this fine old place, so
unlike the mean and cramped externals of English middle
class life, gave the sentiment of a larger and freer existence, and were to me a sort of poetic cultivation, aided also
by the character of the grounds in which the Abbey stood;
which were riant and secluded, umbrageous, and full of
the sound of falling waters.

I owed another of the fortunate circumstances in my
education, a year's residence in France, to Mr. Bentham's
brother, General Sir Samuel Bentham. I had seen Sir
Samuel Bentham and his family at their house near Gos-
port in the course of the tour already mentioned (he being
then Superintendent of the Dockyard at Portsmouth), and
during a stay of a few days which they made at Ford Abbey
shortly after the peace, before going to live on the Continent. In 1820 they invited me for a six months' visit to
them in the South of France, which their kindness ultimately prolonged to nearly a twelvemonth. Sir Samuel
Bentham, though of a character of mind different from that
of his illustrous brother, was a man of very considerable
attainments and general powers, with a decided genius for
mechanical art. His wife, a daughter of the celebrated
chemist, Dr. Fordyce, was a woman of strong will and
decided character, much general knowledge, and great

practical good sense of the Edgeworth kind: she was the
ruling spirit of the household, as she deserved, and was
well qualified, to be. Their family consisted of one son
(the eminent botanist) and three daughters, the youngest
about two years my senior. I am indebted to them for
much and various instruction, and for an almost parental
interest in my welfare. When I first joined them, in May
1820, they occupied the Château of Pompignan (still belonging to a descendant of Voltaire's enemy) on the heights
overlooking the plain of the Garonne between Montauban
and Toulouse. I accompanied them in an excursion to the
Pyrenees, including a stay of some duration at Bagnères
de Bigorre, a journey to Pau, Bayonne, and Bagnères de
Luchon, and an ascent of the Pic du Midi de Bigorre.

This first introduction to the highest order of mountain
scenery made the deepest impression on me, and gave a
colour to my tastes through life. In October we proceeded
by the beautiful mountain route of Castres and St. Pons,
from Toulouse to Montpellier, in which last neighbourhood Sir Samuel had just bought the estate of Restinclière,
near the foot of the singular mountain of St. Loup. During this residence in France I acquired a familiar knowledge
of the French language, and acquaintance with the ordinary
French literature; I took lessons in various bodily exercises,
in none of which however I made any proficiency; and at
Montpellier I attended the excellent winter courses of
lectures at the Faculté des Sciences, those of M. Anglada
on chemistry, of M. Provençal on zoology, and of a very
accomplished representative of the eighteenth century
metaphysics, M. Gergonne, on logic, under the name of
Philosophy of the Sciences. I also went through a course
of the higher mathematics under the private tuition of M.
Lenthéric, a professor at the Lycée of Montpellier. But
the greatest, perhaps, of the many advantages which I
owed to this episode in my education, was that of having
breathed for a whole year, the free and genial atmosphere

of Continental life. This advantage was not the less real though I could not then estimate, nor even consciously feel it. Having so little experience of English life, and the few people I knew being mostly such as had public objects, of a large and personally disinterested kind, at heart, I was ignorant of the low moral tone of what, in England, is called society; the habit of, not indeed professing, but taking for granted in every mode of implication, that conduct is of course always directed towards low and petty objects; the absence of high feelings which manifests itself by sneering depreciation of all demonstrations of them, and by general abstinence (except among a few of the stricter religionists) from professing any high principles of action at all, except in those preordained cases in which such profession is put on as part of the costume and formalities of the occasion. I could not then know or estimate the difference between this manner of existence, and that of a people like the French, whose faults, if equally real, are at all events different; among whom sentiments, which by comparison at least may be called elevated, are the current coin of human intercourse, both in books and in private life; and though often evaporating in profession, are yet kept alive in the nation at large by constant exercise, and stimulated by sympathy, so as to form a living and active part of the existence of great numbers of persons, and to be recognized and understood by all. Neither could I then appreciate the general culture of the understanding, which results from the habitual exercise of the feelings, and is thus carried down into the most uneducated classes of several countries on the Continent, in a degree not equalled in England among the so-called educated, except where an unusual tenderness of conscience leads to a habitual exercise of the intellect on questions of right and wrong. I did not know the way in which, among the ordinary English, the absence of interest in things of an unselfish kind, except occasionally in a special thing here and there, and the habit of not speaking to others, nor much even to themselves, about the things in which they do feel interest, causes both their feelings and their intellectual faculties to remain undeveloped, or to develope themselves only in some single and very limited direction; reducing them, considered as spiritual beings, to a kind of negative existence. All these things I did not perceive till long afterwards; but I even then felt, though without stating it clearly to myself, the contrast between the frank sociability and amiability of French personal intercourse, and the English mode of existence in which everybody acts as if everybody else (with few, or no exceptions) was either an enemy or a bore. In France, it is true, the bad as well as the good points, both of individual and of national character, come more to the surface, and break out more fearlessly in ordinary intercourse, than in England: but the general habit of the people is to show, as well as to expect, friendly feeling in every one towards every other, wherever there is not some positive cause for the opposite. In England it is only of the best bred people, in the upper or upper middle ranks, that anything like this can be said.

In my way through Paris, both going and returning, I passed some time in the house of M. Say, the eminent political economist, who was a friend and correspondent of my father, having become acquainted with him on a visit to England a year or two after the peace. He was a man of the later period of the French Revolution, a fine specimen of the best kind of French Republican, one of those who had never bent the knee to Bonaparte though courted by him to do so; a truly upright, brave, and enlightened man. He lived a quiet and studious life, made happy by warm affections, public and private. He was acquainted with many of the chiefs of the Liberal party, and I saw various noteworthy persons while staying at his house; among whom I have pleasure in the recollection of having once seen Saint-Simon, not yet the founder either of a philosophy or a religion, and considered only as a clever *original*. The chief fruit which I carried away from the society I saw, was a strong and permanent interest in Continental Liberalism, of which I ever afterwards kept myself *au courant*, as much as of English politics: a thing not at all usual in those days with Englishmen, and which had a very salutary influence on my development, keeping me free from the error always prevalent in England, and from which even my father with all his superiority to prejudice was not exempt, of judging universal questions by a merely English standard. After passing a few weeks at Caen with an old friend of my father's, I returned to England in July 1821; and my education resumed its ordinary course.

CHAPTER III

LAST STAGE OF EDUCATION AND FIRST OF
SELF-EDUCATION.

FOR the first year or two after my visit to France, I
continued my old studies, with the addition of some
new ones. When I returned, my father was just finishing
for the press his "Elements of Political Economy," and he
made me perform an exercise on the manuscript, which Mr.
Bentham practised on all his own writings, making what
he called, "marginal contents"; a short abstract of every
paragraph, to enable the writer more easily to judge of,
and improve, the order of the ideas, and the general character of the exposition. Soon after, my father put into my
hands Condillac's Traité des Sensations, and the logical
and metaphysical volumes of his Cours d'Etudes; the first
(notwithstanding the superficial resemblance between Condillac's psychological system and my father's) quite as much
for a warning as for an example. I am not sure whether
it was in this winter or the next that I first read a history
of the French Revolution. I learnt with astonishment,
that the principles of democracy, then apparently in so
insignificant and hopeless a minority everywhere in Europe,
had borne all before them in France thirty years earlier,
and had been the creed of the nation. As may be supposed
from this, I had previously a very vague idea of that great
commotion. I knew only that the French had thrown off
the absolute monarchy of Louis XIV. and XV., had put the
King and Queen to death, guillotined many persons, one
of whom was Lavoisier, and had ultimately fallen under
the despotism of Bonaparte. From this time, as was
natural, the subject took an immense hold of my feelings.

It allied itself with all my juvenile aspirations to the character of a democratic champion. What had happened so lately, seemed as if it might easily happen again: and the most transcendant glory I was capable of conceiving, was that of figuring, successful or unsuccessful, as a Girondist in an English Convention.

During the winter of 1821–2, Mr. John Austin, with whom at the time of my visit to France my father had but lately become acquainted, kindly allowed me to read Roman law with him. My father, notwithstanding his abhorrence of the chaos of barbarism called English Law, had turned his thoughts towards the bar as on the whole less ineligible for me than any other profession: and these readings with Mr. Austin, who had made Bentham's best ideas his own, and added much to them from other sources and from his own mind, were not only a valuable introduction to legal studies, but an important portion of general education. With Mr. Austin I read Heineccius on the Institutes, his Roman Antiquities, and part of his exposition of the Pandects; to which was added a considerable portion of Blackstone. It was at the commencement of these studies that my father, as a needful accompaniment to them, put into my hands Bentham's principal speculations, as interpreted to the Continent, and indeed to all the world, by Dumont, in the Traité de Législation. The reading of this book was an epoch in my life; one of the turning points in my mental history.

My previous education had been, in a certain sense, already a course of Benthamism. The Benthamic standard of " the greatest happiness " was that which I had always been taught to apply; I was even familiar with an abstract discussion of it, forming an episode in an unpublished dialogue on Government, written by my father on the Platonic model. Yet in the first pages of Bentham it burst upon me with all the force of novelty. What thus impressed me was the chapter in which Bentham passed judgment on the common modes of reasoning in morals and legislation, deduced from phrases like " law of nature," " right reason," " the moral sense," " natural rectitude," and the like, and characterized them as dogmatism in disguise, imposing its sentiments upon others under cover of sounding expressions which convey no reason for the sentiment, but set up the sentiment as its own reason.   It had not struck me before, that Bentham's principle put an end to all this.   The feeling rushed upon me, that all previous moralists were superseded, and that here indeed was the commencement of a new era in thought.   This impression was strengthened by the manner in which Bentham put into scientific form the application of the happiness principle to the morality of actions, by analysing the various classes and orders of their consequences.   But what struck me at the time most of all, was the Classification of Offences, which is much more clear, compact and imposing in Dumont's *rédaction* than in the original work of Bentham from which it was taken.   Logic and the dialectics of Plato, which had formed so large a part of my previous training, had given me a strong relish for accurate classification.   This taste had been strengthened and enlightened by the study of botany, on the principles of what is called the Natural Method, which I had taken up with great zeal, though only as an amusement, during my stay in France; and when I found scientific classification applied to the great and complex subject of Punishable Acts, under the guidance of the ethical principle of Pleasurable and Painful Consequences, followed out in the method of detail introduced into these subjects by Bentham, I felt taken up to an eminence from which I could survey a vast mental domain, and see stretching out into the distance intellectual results beyond all computation.   As I proceeded further, there seemed to be added to this intellectual clearness, the most inspiring prospects of practical improvements in human affairs.   To Bentham's general view of the construction of a body of law I was not altogether a stranger, having read with attention that admirable compendium, my father's article " Jurisprudence ": but I had read it with little profit and scarcely any interest, no doubt from its extremely general and abstract character, and also because it concerned the form more than the substance of the *corpus juris*, the logic rather than the ethics of law. But Bentham's subject was Legislation, of which Jurisprudence is only the formal part: and at every page he seemed to open a clearer and broader conception of what human opinions and institutions ought to be, how they might be made what they ought to be, and how far removed from it they now are. When I laid down the last volume of the Traité, I had become a different being. The "principle of utility" understood as Bentham understood it, and applied in the manner in which he applied it through these three volumes, fell exactly into its place as the keystone which held together the detached and fragmentary component parts of my knowledge and beliefs. It gave unity to my conceptions of things. I now had opinions; a creed, a doctrine, a philosophy; in one among the best senses of the word, a religion; the inculcation and diffusion of which could be made the principal outward purpose of a life. And I had a grand conception laid before me of changes to be effected in the condition of mankind through that doctrine. The Traité de Législation wound up with what was to me a most impressive picture of human life as it would be made by such opinions and such laws as were recommended in the treatise. The anticipations of practicable improvement were studiously moderate, deprecating and discountenancing as reveries of vague enthusiasm many things which will one day seem so natural to human beings, that injustice will probably be done to those who once thought them chimerical. But, in my state of mind, this appearance of superiority to illusion added to the effect which Bentham's doctrines produced on me, by heightening the impression of mental power, and the vista of improvement which he did open was sufficiently large and brilliant to light up my life, as well as to give a definite shape to my aspirations.

After this I read, from time to time, the most important of the other works of Bentham which had then seen the light, either as written by himself or as edited by Dumont. This was my private reading: while, under my father's direction, my studies were carried into the higher branches of analytic psychology. I now read Locke's Essay, and wrote out an account of it, consisting of a complete abstract of every chapter, with such remarks as occurred to me: which was read by, or (I think) to, my father, and discussed throughout. I performed the same process with Helvetius de l'Esprit, which I read of my own choice. This preparation of abstracts, subject to my father's censorship, was of great service to me, by compelling precision in conceiving and expressing psychological doctrines, whether accepted as truths or only regarded as the opinion of others. After Helvetius, my father made me study what he deemed the really master-production in the philosophy of mind, Hartley's Observations on Man. This book, though it did not, like the Traité de Législation, give a new colour to my existence, made a very similar impression on me in regard to its immediate subject. Hartley's explanation, incomplete as in many points it is, of the more complex mental phenomena by the law of association, commended itself to me at once as a real analysis, and made me feel by contrast the insufficiency of the merely verbal generalizations of Condillac, and even of the instructive gropings and feelings about for psychological explanations, of Locke. It was at this very time that my father commenced writing his Analysis of the Mind, which carried Hartley's mode of explaining the mental phenomena to so much greater length and depth. He could only command the concentration of thought necessary for this work, during the complete leisure of his holiday of a month or six weeks annually: and he commenced it in the summer of 1822, in the first holiday he passed at Dorking; in which neighbourhood, from that time to the end of his life, with the exception of two years, he lived, as far as his official duties permitted, for six months of every year. He worked at the Analysis during several successive vacations, up to the year 1829 when it was published, and allowed me to read the manuscript, portion by portion, as it advanced. The other principal English writers on mental philosophy I read as I felt inclined, particularly Berkeley, Hume's Essays, Reid, Dugald Stewart and Brown on Cause and Effect. Brown's Lectures I did not read until two or three years later, nor at that time had my father himself read them.

Among the works read in the course of this year, which contributed materially to my development, I ought to mention a book (written on the foundation of some of Bentham's manuscripts and published under the pseudonyme of Philip Beauchamp) entitled " Analysis of the Influence of Natural Religion on the Temporal Happiness of Mankind." This was an examination not of the truth, but of the usefulness of religious belief, in the most general sense, apart from the peculiarities of any special Revelation; which, of all the parts of the discussion concerning religion, is the most important in this age, in which real belief in any religious doctrine is feeble and precarious, but the opinion of its necessity for moral and social purposes almost universal; and when those who reject revelation, very generally take refuge in an optimistic Deism, a worship of the order of Nature, and the supposed course of Providence, at least as full of contradictions, and perverting to the moral sentiments, as any of the forms of Christianity, if only it is as completely realized. Yet, very little, with any claim to a philosophical character, has been written by sceptics against the usefulness of this form of belief. The volume bearing the name of Philip Beauchamp had this for its special object. Having been shown to my father in manuscript, it was put into my hands by him, and I made a marginal analysis of it as I had done of the Elements of Political Economy. Next to the Traité de Législation, it was one of the books which by the searching character of its analysis produced the greatest effect upon me. On reading it lately after an interval of many years, I find it to have some of the defects as well as the merits of the Benthamic modes of thought, and to contain, as I now think, many weak arguments, but with a great overbalance of sound ones, and much good material for a more completely philosophic and conclusive treatment of the subject.

I have now, I believe, mentioned all the books which had any considerable effect on my early mental development. From this point I began to carry on my intellectual cultivation by writing still more than by reading. In the summer of 1822 I wrote my first argumentative essay. I remember very little about it, except that it was an attack on what I regarded as the aristocratic prejudice, that the rich were, or were likely to be, superior in moral qualities to the poor. My performance was entirely argumentative, without any of the declamation which the subject would admit of, and might be expected to suggest to a young writer. In that department however I was, and remained, very inapt. Dry argument was the only thing I could manage, or willingly attempted; though passively I was very susceptible to the effect of all composition, whether in the form of poetry or oratory, which appealed to the feelings on any basis of reason. My father, who knew nothing of this essay until it was finished, was well satisfied, and as I learnt from others, even pleased with it; but, perhaps from a desire to promote the exercise of other mental faculties than the purely logical, he advised me to make my next exercise in composition one of the oratorical kind: on which suggestion, availing myself of my familiarity with Greek history and ideas and with the Athenian orators,

I wrote two speeches, one an accusation, the other a defence of Pericles, on a supposed impeachment for not marching out to fight the Lacedæmonians on their invasion of Attica. After this I continued to write papers on subjects often very much beyond my capacity, but with great benefit both from the exercise itself, and from the discussions which it led to with my father.

I had now also begun to converse, on general subjects, with the instructed men with whom I came in contact: and the opportunities of such contact naturally became more numerous. The two friends of my father from whom I derived most, and with whom I most associated, were Mr. Grote and Mr. John Austin. The acquaintance of both with my father was recent, but had ripened rapidly into intimacy. Mr. Grote was introduced to my father by Mr. Ricardo, I think in 1819, (being then about twenty-five years old), and sought assiduously his society and conversation. Already a highly instructed man, he was yet, by the side of my father, a tyro on the great subjects of human opinion; but he rapidly seized on my father's best ideas; and in the department of political opinion he made himself known as early as 1820, by a pamphlet in defence of Radical Reform, in reply to a celebrated article by Sir James Mackintosh, then lately published in the Edinburgh Review. Mr. Grote's father, the banker, was, I believe, a thorough Tory, and his mother intensely Evangelical; so that for his liberal opinions he was in no way indebted to home influences. But, unlike most persons who have the prospect of being rich by inheritance, he had, though actively engaged in the business of banking, devoted a great portion of time to philosophic studies; and his intimacy with my father did much to decide the character of the next stage in his mental progress. Him I often visited, and my conversations with him on political, moral, and philosophical subjects gave me, in addition to much valuable instruction, all the pleasure and benefit of sympathetic communion with a man of the high intellectual and moral eminence which his life and writings have since manifested to the world.

Mr. Austin, who was four or five years older than Mr. Grote, was the eldest son of a retired miller in Suffolk, who had made money by contracts during the war, and who must have been a man of remarkable qualities, as I infer from the fact that all his sons were of more than common ability and all eminently gentlemen. The one with whom we are now concerned, and whose writings on jurisprudence have made him celebrated, was for some time in the army, and served in Sicily under Lord William Bentinck. After the peace he sold his commission and studied for the bar, to which he had been called for some time before my father knew him. He was not, like Mr. Grote, to any extent a pupil of my father, but he had attained, by reading and thought, a considerable number of the same opinions, modified by his own very decided individuality of character. He was a man of great intellectual powers which in conversation appeared at their very best; from the vigour and richness of expression with which, under the excitement of discussion, he was accustomed to maintain some view or other of most general subjects; and from an appearance of not only strong, but deliberate and collected will; mixed with a certain bitterness, partly derived from temperament, and partly from the general cast of his feelings and reflexions. The dissatisfaction with life and the world, felt more or less in the present state of society and intellect by every discerning and highly conscientious mind, gave in his case a rather melancholy tinge to the character, very natural to those whose passive moral susceptibilities are more than proportioned to their active energies. For it must be said, that the strength of will of which his manner seemed to give such strong assurance, expended itself principally in manner. With great zeal for human improvement, a strong sense of duty, and capacities and acquirements the extent of which is proved by the writings he has left, he hardly ever completed any intellectual task of magnitude. He had so high a standard of what ought to be done, so exaggerated a sense of deficiencies in his own performances, and was so unable to content himself with the amount of elaboration sufficient for the occasion and the purpose, that he not only spoilt much of his work for ordinary use by overlabouring it, but spent so much time and exertion in superfluous study and thought, that when his task ought to have been completed, he had generally worked himself into an illness, without having half finished what he undertook. From this mental infirmity (of which he is not the sole example among the accomplished and able men whom I have known), combined with liability to frequent attacks of disabling though not dangerous ill-health, he accomplished, through life, little in comparison with what he seemed capable of; but what he did produce is held in the very highest estimation by the most competent judges; and, like Coleridge, he might plead as a set-off that he had been to many persons, through his conversation, a source not only of much instruction but of great elevation of character. On me his influence was most salutary. It was moral in the best sense. He took a sincere and kind interest in me, far beyond what could have been expected towards a mere youth from a man of his age, standing, and what seemed austerity of character. There was in his conversation and demeanour a tone of highmindedness which did not show itself so much, if the quality existed as much, in any of the other persons with whom at that time I associated. My intercourse with him was the more beneficial, owing to his being of a different mental type from all other intellectual men whom I frequented, and he from the first set himself decidedly against the prejudices and narrownesses which are almost sure to be found in a young man formed by a particular mode of thought or a particular social circle.

His younger brother, Charles Austin, of whom at this time and for the next year or two I saw much, had also a great effect on me, though of a very different description. He was but a few years older than myself, and had then just left the University, where he had shone with great éclat as a man of intellect and a brilliant orator and converser. The effect he produced on his Cambridge contemporaries deserves to be accounted an historical event; for to it may in part be traced the tendency towards Liberalism in general, and the Benthamic and politico-economic form of it in particular, which showed itself in a portion of the more active-minded young men of the higher classes from this time to 1830. The Union Debating Society, at that time at the height of its reputation, was an arena where what were then thought extreme opinions, in politics and philosophy, were weekly asserted, face to face with their opposites, before audiences consisting of the élite of the Cambridge youth: and though many persons afterwards of more or less note, (of whom Lord Macaulay is the most celebrated), gained their first oratorical laurels in those debates, the really influential mind among these intellectual gladiators was Charles Austin. He continued, after leaving the University, to be, by his conversation and personal ascendancy, a leader among the same class of young men who had been his associates there; and he attached me among others to his car. Through him I became acquainted with Macaulay, Hyde and Charles Villiers, Strutt (now Lord Belper), Romilly (now Lord Romilly and Master of the Rolls), and various others who subsequently figured in literature or politics, and among whom I heard discussions on many topics, as yet to a certain degree new to me. The influence of Charles Austin over me differed from that of the persons I have hitherto mentioned, in being not the influence of a man over a boy, but that of an elder contemporary. It was through him that I first felt myself, not a pupil under teachers, but a man

among men. He was the first person of intellect whom I
met on a ground of equality, though as yet much his inferior on that common ground. He was a man who never
failed to impress greatly those with whom he came in
contact, even when their opinions were the very reverse of
his. The impression he gave was that of boundless
strength, together with talents which, combined with such
apparent force of will and character, seemed capable of
dominating the world. Those who knew him, whether
friendly to him or not, always anticipated that he would
play a conspicuous part in public life. It is seldom that
men produce so great an immediate effect by speech, unless
they, in some degree, lay themselves out for it; and he
did this in no ordinary degree. He loved to strike, and
even to startle. He knew that decision is the greatest
element of effect, and he uttered his opinions with all the
decision he could throw into them, never so well pleased
as when he astonished any one by their audacity. Very
unlike his brother, who made war against the narrower
interpretations and applications of the principles they both
professed, he, on the contrary, presented the Benthamic
doctrines in the most startling form of which they were
susceptible, exaggerating everything in them which tended
to consequences offensive to any one's preconceived feelings. All which, he defended with such verve and vivacity,
and carried off by a manner so agreeable as well as forcible,
that he always either came off victor, or divided the honours
of the field. It is my belief that much of the notion
popularly entertained of the tenets and sentiments of what
are called Benthamites or Utilitarians had its origin in
paradoxes thrown out by Charles Austin. It must be said,
however, that his example was followed, *haud passibus
æquis*, by younger proselytes, and that to *outrer* whatever was by anybody considered offensive in the doctrines
and maxims of Benthamism, became at one time the badge
of a small coterie of youths. All of these who had any-

thing in them, myself among others, quickly outgrew this boyish vanity; and those who had not, became tired of differing from other people, and gave up both the good and the bad part of the heterodox opinions they had for some time professed.

It was in the winter of 1822–3 that I formed the plan of a little society, to be composed of young men agreeing in fundamental principles — acknowledging Utility as their standard in ethics and politics, and a certain number of the principal corollaries drawn from it in the philosophy I had accepted — and meeting once a fortnight to read essays and discuss questions conformably to the premises thus agreed on. The fact would hardly be worth mentioning, but for the circumstance, that the name I gave to the society I had planned was the Utilitarian Society. It was the first time that any one had taken the title of Utilitarian; and the term made its way into the language from this humble source. I did not invent the word, but found it in one of Galt's novels, the "Annals of the Parish," in which the Scotch clergyman, of whom the book is a supposed autobiography, is represented as warning his parishioners not to leave the Gospel and become utilitarians. With a boy's fondness for a name and a banner I seized on the word, and for some years called myself and others by it as a sectarian appellation; and it came to be occasionally used by some others holding the opinions which it was intended to designate. As those opinions attracted more notice, the term was repeated by strangers and opponents, and got into rather common use just about the time when those who had originally assumed it, laid down that along with other sectarian characteristics. The Society so called consisted at first of no more than three members, one of whom, being Mr. Bentham's amanuensis, obtained for us permission to hold our meetings in his house. The number never, I think, reached ten, and the society was broken up in 1826. It had thus an existence of about three years and a half. The chief effect of it as regards myself, over and above the benefit of practice in oral discussion, was that of bringing me in contact with several young men at that time less advanced than myself, among whom, as they professed the same opinions, I was for some time a sort of leader, and had considerable influence on their mental progress. Any young man of education who fell in my way, and whose opinions were not incompatible with those of the Society, I endeavoured to press into its service; and some others I probably should never have known, had they not joined it. Those of the members who became my intimate companions — no one of whom was in any sense of the word a disciple, but all of them independent thinkers on their own basis — were William Eyton Tooke, son of the eminent political economist, a young man of singular worth both moral and intellectual, lost to the world by an early death; his friend William Ellis, an original thinker in the field of political economy, now honourably known by his apostolic exertions for the improvement of education; George Graham, afterwards an official assignee of the Bankruptcy Court, a thinker of originality and power on almost all abstract subjects; and (from the time when he came first to England to study for the bar in 1824 or 1825) a man who has made considerably more noise in the world than any of these, John Arthur Roebuck.

In May, 1823, my professional occupation and status for the next thirty-five years of my life, were decided by my father's obtaining for me an appointment from the East India Company, in the office of the Examiner of India Correspondence, immediately under himself. I was appointed in the usual manner, at the bottom of the list of clerks, to rise, at least in the first instance, by seniority; but with the understanding that I should be employed from the beginning in preparing drafts of despatches, and be thus trained up as a successor to those who then filled the

higher departments of the office. My drafts of course
required, for some time, much revision from my immediate
superiors, but I soon became well acquainted with the business, and by my father's instructions and the general growth
of my own powers, I was in a few years qualified to be,
and practically was, the chief conductor of the correspondence with India in one of the leading departments, that of
the Native States. This continued to be my official duty
until I was appointed Examiner, only two years before the
time when the abolition of the East India Company as a
political body determined my retirement. I do not know
any one of the occupations by which a subsistence can now
be gained, more suitable than such as this to any one who,
not being in independent circumstances, desires to devote a
part of the twenty-four hours to private intellectual pursuits. Writing for the press, cannot be recommended as
a permanent resource to any one qualified to accomplish
anything in the higher departments of literature or
thought: not only on account of the uncertainty of this
means of livelihood, especially if the writer has a conscience, and will not consent to serve any opinions except
his own; but also because the writings by which one can
live, are not the writings which themselves live, and are
never those in which the writer does his best. Books destined to form future thinkers take too much time to write,
and when written come, in general, too slowly into notice
and repute, to be relied on for subsistence. Those who
have to support themselves by their pen must depend on
literary drudgery, or at best on writings addressed to the
multitude; and can employ in the pursuits of their own
choice, only such time as they can spare from those of
necessity; which is generally less than the leisure allowed
by office occupations, while the effect on the mind is far
more enervating and fatiguing. For my own part I have,
through life, found office duties an actual rest from the
other mental occupations which I have carried on simultaneously with them. They were sufficiently intellectual

not to be a distasteful drudgery, without being such as to cause any strain upon the mental powers of a person used to abstract thought, or to the labour of careful literary composition. The drawbacks, for every mode of life has its drawbacks, were not, however, unfelt by me. I cared little for the loss of the chances of riches and honours held out by some of the professions, particularly the bar, which had been, as I have already said, the profession thought of for me. But I was not indifferent to exclusion from Parliament, and public life: and I felt very sensibly the more immediate unpleasantness of confinement to London; the holiday allowed by India-house practice not exceeding a month in the year, while my taste was strong for a country life, and my sojourn in France had left behind it an ardent desire of travelling. But though these tastes could not be freely indulged, they were at no time entirely sacrificed. I passed most Sundays, throughout the year, in the country, taking long rural walks on that day even when residing in London. The month's holiday was, for a few years, passed at my father's house in the country: afterwards a part or the whole was spent in tours, chiefly pedestrian, with some one or more of the young men who were my chosen companions; and, at a later period, in longer journeys or excursions, alone or with other friends. France, Belgium, and Rhenish Germany were within easy reach of the annual holiday: and two longer absences, one of three, the other of six months, under medical advice, added Switzerland, the Tyrol, and Italy to my list. Fortunately, also, both these journeys occurred rather early, so as to give the benefit and charm of the remembrance to a large portion of life.

I am disposed to agree with what has been surmised by others, that the opportunity which my official position gave me of learning by personal observation the necessary conditions of the practical conduct of public affairs, has been of considerable value to me as a theoretical reformer of the opinions and institutions of my time. Not, indeed, that public business transacted on paper, to take effect on the other side of the globe, was of itself calculated to give much practical knowledge of life. But the occupation accustomed me to see and hear the difficulties of every course, and the means of obviating them, stated and discussed deliberately with a view to execution; it gave me opportunities of perceiving when public measures, and other political facts, did not produce the effects which had been expected of them, and from what causes; above all, it was valuable to me by making me, in this portion of my activity, merely one wheel in a machine, the whole of which had to work together. As a speculative writer, I should have had no one to consult but myself, and should have encountered in my speculations none of the obstacles which would have started up whenever they came to be applied to practice. But as a Secretary conducting political correspondence, I could not issue an order or express an opinion, without satisfying various persons very unlike myself, that the thing was fit to be done. I was thus in a good position for finding out by practice the mode of putting a thought which gives it easiest admittance into minds not prepared for it by habit; while I became practically conversant with the difficulties of moving bodies of men, the necessities of compromise, the art of sacrificing the non-essential to preserve the essential. I learnt how to obtain the best I could, when I could not obtain everything; instead of being indignant or dispirited because I could not have entirely my own way, to be pleased and encouraged when I could have the smallest part of it; and when even that could not be, to bear with complete equanimity the being overruled altogether. I have found, through life, these acquisitions to be of the greatest possible importance for personal happiness, and they are also a very necessary condition for enabling any one, either as theorist or as practical man, to effect the greatest amount of good compatible with his opportunities.

Chapter IV

YOUTHFUL PROPAGANDISM.   THE WEST-
MINSTER REVIEW.

THE occupation of so much of my time by office work
did not relax my attention to my own pursuits, which
were never carried on more vigorously. It was about this
time that I began to write in newspapers. The first writings of mine which got into print were two letters published
towards the end of 1822, in the Traveller evening newspaper. The Traveller (which afterwards grew into the
" Globe and Traveller," by the purchase and incorporation
of the Globe) was then the property of the well-known
political economist, Colonel Torrens, and under the
editorship of an able man, Mr. Walter Coulson (who,
after being an amanuensis of Mr. Bentham, became a
reporter, then an editor, next a barrister and conveyancer,
and died Counsel to the Home Office), it had become one
of the most important newspaper organs of liberal politics.
Col. Torrens himself wrote much of the political economy
of his paper; and had at this time made an attack upon
some opinion of Ricardo and my father, to which, at my
father's instigation, I attempted an answer, and Coulson,
out of consideration for my father and goodwill to me,
inserted it. There was a reply by Torrens, to which I
again rejoined. I soon after attempted something considerably more ambitious. The prosecutions of Richard
Carlile and his wife and sister for publications hostile to
Christianity, were then exciting much attention, and no-
where more than among the people I frequented. Freedom of discussion even in politics, much more in religion,
was at that time far from being, even in theory, the con-

ceded point which it at least seems to be now; and the holders of obnoxious opinions had to be always ready to argue and re-argue for the liberty of expressing them. I wrote a series of five letters, under the signature of Wickliffe, going over the whole length and breadth of the question of free publication of all opinions on religion, and offered them to the Morning Chronicle. Three of them were published in January and February, 1823; the other two, containing things too outspoken for that journal, never appeared at all. But a paper which I wrote soon after on the same subject, *à propos* of a debate in the House of Commons, was inserted as a leading article; and during the whole of this year, 1823, a considerable number of my contributions were printed in the Chronicle and Traveller: sometimes notices of books but oftener letters, commenting on some nonsense talked in Parliament, or some defect of the law, or misdoings of the magistracy or the courts of justice. In this last department the Chronicle was now rendering signal service. After the death of Mr. Perry, the editorship and management of the paper had devolved on Mr. John Black, long a reporter on its establishment; a man of most extensive reading and information, great honesty and simplicity of mind; a particular friend of my father, imbued with many of his and Bentham's ideas, which he reproduced in his articles, among other valuable thoughts, with great facility and skill. From this time the Chronicle ceased to be the merely Whig organ it was before, and during the next ten years became to a considerable extent a vehicle of the opinions of the Utilitarian radicals. This was mainly by what Black himself wrote, with some assistance from Fonblanque, who first showed his eminent qualities as a writer by articles and *jeux d'esprit* in the Chronicle. The defects of the law, and of the administration of justice, were the subject on which that paper rendered most service to improvement. Up to that time hardly a word had been said, except by Bentham and my father, against that most peccant part of English institutions and of their administration. It was the almost universal creed of Englishmen, that the law of England, the judicature of England, the unpaid magistracy of England, were models of excellence. I do not go beyond the mark in saying, that after Bentham, who supplied the principal materials, the greatest share of the merit of breaking down this wretched superstition belongs to Black, as editor of the Morning Chronicle. He kept up an incessant fire against it, exposing the absurdities and vices of the law and the courts of justice, paid and unpaid, until he forced some sense of them into people's minds. On many other questions he became the organ of opinions much in advance of any which had ever before found regular advocacy in the newspaper press. Black was a frequent visitor of my father, and Mr. Grote used to say that he always knew by the Monday morning's article, whether Black had been with my father on the Sunday. Black was one of the most influential of the many channels through which my father's conversation and personal influence made his opinions tell on the world; co-operating with the effect of his writings in making him a power in the country, such as it has rarely been the lot of an individual in a private station to be, through the mere force of intellect and character: and a power which was often acting the most efficiently where it was least seen and suspected. I have already noticed how much of what was done by Ricardo, Hume, and Grote, was the result, in part, of his prompting and persuasion. He was the good genius by the side of Brougham in most of what he did for the public, either on education, law reform, or any other subject. And his influence flowed in minor streams too numerous to be specified. This influence was now about to receive a great extension by the foundation of the Westminster Review.

Contrary to what may have been supposed, my father was in no degree a party to setting up the Westminster

Review. The need of a Radical organ to make head against the Edinburgh and Quarterly (then in the period of their greatest reputation and influence), had been a topic of conversation between him and Mr. Bentham many years earlier, and it had been a part of their *château en Espagne* that my father should be the editor; but the idea had never assumed any practical shape. In 1823, however, Mr. Bentham determined to establish the review at his own cost, and offered the editorship to my father, who declined it as incompatible with his India House appointment. It was then entrusted to Mr. (now Sir John) Bowring, at that time a merchant in the City. Mr. Bowring had been for two or three years previous an assiduous frequenter of Mr. Bentham, to whom he was recommended by many personal good qualities, by an ardent admiration for Bentham, a zealous adoption of many, though not all, of his opinions, and, not least, by an extensive acquaintanceship and correspondence with Liberals of all countries, which seemed to qualify him for being a powerful agent in spreading Bentham's fame and doctrines through all quarters of the world. My father had seen little of Bowring, but knew enough of him to have formed a strong opinion, that he was a man of an entirely different type from what my father considered suitable for conducting a political and philosophical review: and he augured so ill of the enterprise that he regretted it altogether, feeling persuaded not only that Mr. Bentham would lose his money, but that discredit would probably be brought upon radical principles. He could not, however, desert Mr. Bentham, and he consented to write an article for the first number. As it had been a favourite portion of the scheme formerly talked of, that part of the work should be devoted to reviewing the other Reviews, this article of my father's was to be a general criticism of the Edinburgh Review from its commencement. Before writing it he made me read through all the volumes of the Review, or as much of each as seemed of any importance (which was not so arduous a task in 1823 as it would be now), and make notes for him of the articles which I thought he would wish to examine, either on account of their good or their bad qualities. This paper of my father's was the chief cause of the sensation which the Westminster Review produced at its first appearance, and is, both in conception and in execution, one of the most striking of all his writings. He began by an analysis of the tendencies of periodical literature in general; pointing out, that it cannot, like books, wait for success, but must succeed immediately, or not at all, and is hence almost certain to profess and inculcate the opinions already held by the public to which it addresses itself, instead of attempting to rectify or improve those opinions. He next, to characterize the position of the Edinburgh Review as a political organ, entered into a complete analysis, from the Radical point of view, of the British Constitution. He held up to notice its thoroughly aristocratic character: the nomination of a majority of the House of Commons by a few hundred families; the entire identification of the more independent portion, the county members, with the great landholders; the different classes whom this narrow oligarchy was induced, for convenience, to admit to a share of power; and finally, what he called its two props, the Church, and the legal profession. He pointed out the natural tendency of an aristocratic body of this composition, to group itself into two parties, one of them in possession of the executive, the other endeavouring to supplant the former and become the predominant section by the aid of public opinion, without any essential sacrifice of the aristocratic predominance. He described the course likely to be pursued, and the political ground occupied, by an aristocratic party in opposition, coquetting with popular principles for the sake of popular support. He showed how this idea was realized in the conduct of the Whig party, and of the Edinburgh Review as its chief literary organ. He

described, as their main characteristic, what he termed
" seesaw; " writing alternately on both sides of every question which touched the power or interest of the governing
classes; sometimes in different articles, sometimes in different parts of the same article: and illustrated his position
by copious specimens. So formidable an attack on the
Whig party and policy had never before been made; nor
had so great a blow been ever struck, in this country, for
radicalism; nor was there, I believe, any living person
capable of writing that article, except my father.[1]

In the meantime the nascent review had formed a junction with another project, of a purely literary periodical, to
be edited by Mr. Henry Southern, afterwards a diploma-
tist, then a literary man by profession. The two editors
agreed to unite their corps, and divide the editorship, Bowring taking the political, Southern the literary department.
Southern's review was to have been published by Longman, and that firm, though part proprietors of the Edinburgh, were willing to be the publishers of the new journal.
But when all the arrangements had been made, and the
prospectuses sent out, the Longmans saw my father's attack
on the Edinburgh, and drew back. My father was now
appealed to for his interest with his own publisher, Baldwin, which was exerted with a successful result. And so,
in April, 1824, amidst anything but hope on my father's
part, and that of most of those who afterwards aided in
carrying on the review, the first number made its appearance.

That number was an agreeable surprise to most of us.
The average of the articles was of much better quality than
had been expected. The literary and artistic department
had rested chiefly on Mr. Bingham, a barrister (subse-

---

[1] The continuation of this article in the second number of the review
was written by me under my father's eye, and (except as practice in
composition, in which respect it was, to me, more useful than anything
else I ever wrote) was of little or no value.

quently a Police Magistrate), who had been for some years a frequenter of Bentham, was a friend of both the Austins, and had adopted with great ardour Mr. Bentham's philosophical opinions. Partly from accident, there were in the first number as many as five articles by Bingham; and we were extremely pleased with them. I well remember the mixed feeling I myself had about the Review; the joy at finding, what we did not at all expect, that it was sufficiently good to be capable of being made a creditable organ of those who held the opinions it professed; and extreme vexation, since it was so good on the whole, at what we thought the blemishes of it. When, however, in addition to our generally favourable opinion of it, we learned that it had an extraordinarily large sale for a first number, and found that the appearance of a Radical review, with pretensions equal to those of the established organs of parties, had excited much attention, there could be no room for hesitation, and we all became eager in doing everything we could to strengthen and improve it.

My father continued to write occasional articles. The Quarterly Review received its exposure, as a sequel to that of the Edinburgh. Of his other contributions, the most important were an attack on Southey's Book of the Church, in the fifth number, and a political article in the twelfth. Mr. Austin only contributed one paper, but one of great merit, an argument against primogeniture, in reply to an article then lately published in the Edinburgh Review by M\`Culloch. Grote also was a contributor only once; all the time he could spare being already taken up with his History of Greece. The article he wrote was on his own subject, and was a very complete exposure and castigation of Mitford. Bingham and Charles Austin continued to write for some time; Fonblanque was a frequent contributor from the third number. Of my particular associates, Ellis was a regular writer up to the ninth number; and about the time when he left off, others of the set began; Eyton

Tooke, Graham, and Roebuck. I was myself the most frequent writer of all, having contributed, from the second number to the eighteenth, thirteen articles; reviews of books on history and political economy, or discussions on special political topics, as corn laws, game laws, laws of libel. Occasional articles of merit came in from other acquaintances of my father's, and, in time, of mine; and some of Mr. Bowring's writers turned out well. On the whole, however, the conduct of the Review was never satisfactory to any of the persons strongly interested in its principles, with whom I came in contact. Hardly ever did a number come out without containing several things extremely offensive to us, either in point of opinion, of taste, or by mere want of ability. The unfavourable judgments passed by my father, Grote, the two Austins, and others, were re-echoed with exaggeration by us younger people; and as our youthful zeal rendered us by no means backward in making complaints, we led the two editors a sad life. From my knowledge of what I then was, I have no doubt that we were at least as often wrong as right; and I am very certain that if the Review had been carried on according to our notions (I mean those of the juniors), it would have been no better, perhaps not even so good as it was. But it is worth noting as a fact in the history of Benthamism, that the periodical organ, by which it was best known, was from the first extremely unsatisfactory to those whose opinions on all subjects it was supposed specially to represent.

Meanwhile, however, the Review made considerable noise in the world, and gave a recognised *status*, in the arena of opinion and discussion, to the Benthamic type of radicalism, out of all proportion to the number of its adherents, and to the personal merits and abilities, at that time, of most of those who could be reckoned among them. It was a time, as is known, of rapidly rising Liberalism. When the fears and animosities accompanying the war with

France had been brought to an end, and people had once more a place in their thoughts for home politics, the tide began to set towards reform. The renewed oppression of the Continent by the old reigning families, the countenance apparently given by the English Government to the conspiracy against liberty called the Holy Alliance, and the enormous weight of the national debt and taxation occasioned by so long and costly a war, rendered the government and parliament very unpopular. Radicalism, under the leadership of the Burdetts and Cobbetts, had assumed a character and importance which seriously alarmed the Administration: and their alarm had scarcely been temporarily assuaged by the celebrated Six Acts, when the trial of Queen Caroline roused a still wider and deeper feeling of hatred. Though the outward signs of this hatred passed away with its exciting cause, there arose on all sides a spirit which had never shown itself before, of opposition to abuses in detail. Mr. Hume's persevering scrutiny of the public expenditure, forcing the House of Commons to a division on every objectionable item in the estimates, had begun to tell with great force on public opinion, and had extorted many minor retrenchments from an unwilling administration. Political economy had asserted itself with great vigour in public affairs, by the Petition of the Merchants of London for Free Trade, drawn up in 1820 by Mr. Tooke and presented by Mr. Alexander Baring; and by the noble exertions of Ricardo during the few years of his parliamentary life. His writings, following up the impulse given by the Bullion controversy, and followed up in their turn by the expositions and comments of my father and McCulloch (whose writings in the Edinburgh Review during those years were most valuable), had drawn general attention to the subject, making at least partial converts in the Cabinet itself; and Huskisson, supported by Canning, had commenced that gradual demolition of the protective system, which one of

their colleagues virtually completed in 1846, though the
last vestiges were only swept away by Mr. Gladstone in
1860. Mr. Peel, then Home Secretary, was entering
cautiously into the untrodden and peculiarly Benthamic
path of Law Reform. At this period, when Liberalism
seemed to be becoming the tone of the time, when improvement of institutions was preached from the highest places,
and a complete change of the constitution of Parliament
was loudly demanded in the lowest, it is not strange that
attention should have been roused by the regular appearance in controversy of what seemed a new school of writers,
claiming to be the legislators and theorists of this new
tendency. The air of strong conviction with which they
wrote, when scarcely any one else seemed to have an equally
strong faith in as definite a creed; the boldness with which
they tilted against the very front of both the existing
political parties; their uncompromising profession of opposition to many of the generally received opinions, and the
suspicion they lay under of holding others still more heterodox than they professed; the talent and verve of at least
my father's articles, and the appearance of a corps behind
him sufficient to carry on a review; and finally, the fact
that the review was bought and read, made the so-called
Bentham school in philosophy and politics fill a greater
place in the public mind than it had held before, or has
ever again held since other equally earnest schools of
thought have arisen in England. As I was in the head-
quarters of it, knew of what it was composed, and as one
of the most active of its very small number, might say
without undue assumption, *quorum pars magna fui*, it belongs to me more than to most others, to give some account
of it.

This supposed school, then, had no other existence than
what was constituted by the fact, that my father's writings
and conversation drew round him a certain number of young
men who had already imbibed, or who imbibed from him,

a greater or smaller portion of his very decided political and philosophical opinions. The notion that Bentham was surrounded by a band of disciples who received their opinions from his lips, is a fable to which my father did justice in his " Fragment on Mackintosh," and which, to all who knew Mr. Bentham's habits of life and manner of conversation, is simply ridiculous. The influence which Bentham exercised was by his writings. Through them he has produced, and is producing, effects on the condition of mankind, wider and deeper, no doubt, than any which can be attributed to my father. He is a much greater name in history. But my father exercised a far greater personal ascendancy. He *was* sought for the vigour and instructiveness of his conversation, and did use it largely as an instrument for the diffusion of his opinions. I have never known any man who could do such ample justice to his best thoughts in colloquial discussion. His perfect command over his great mental resources, the terseness and expressiveness of his language and the moral earnestness as well as intellectual force of his delivery, made him one of the most striking of all argumentative conversers: and he was full of anecdote, a hearty laugher, and, when with people whom he liked, a most lively and amusing companion. It was not solely, or even chiefly, in diffusing his merely intellectual convictions that his power showed itself: it was still more through the influence of a quality, of which I have only since learnt to appreciate the extreme rarity: that exalted public spirit, and regard above all things to the good of the whole, which warmed into life and activity every germ of similar virtue that existed in the minds he came in contact with: the desire he made them feel for his approbation, the shame at his disapproval; the moral support which his conversation and his very existence gave to those who were aiming to the same objects, and the encouragement he afforded to the fainthearted or desponding among them, by the firm confidence which (though the reverse of sanguine as to the results to be expected in any one particular case) he always felt in the power of reason, the general progress of improvement, and the good which individuals could do by judicious effort.

It was my father's opinions which gave the distinguishing character to the Benthamic or utilitarian propagandism of that time. They fell singly, scattered from him in many directions, but they flowed from him in a continued stream principally in three channels. One was through me, the only mind directly formed by his instructions, and through whom considerable influence was exercised over various young men, who became, in their turn, propagandists. A second was through some of the Cambridge contemporaries of Charles Austin, who, either initiated by him or under the general mental impulse which he gave, had adopted many opinions allied to those of my father, and some of the more considerable of whom afterwards sought my father's acquaintance and frequented his house. Among these may be mentioned Strutt, afterwards Lord Belper, and the present Lord Romilly, with whose eminent father, Sir Samuel, my father had of old been on terms of friendship. The third channel was that of a younger generation of Cambridge undergraduates, contemporary, not with Austin, but with Eyton Tooke, who were drawn to that estimable person by affinity of opinions, and introduced by him to my father: the most notable of these was Charles Buller. Various other persons individually received and transmitted a considerable amount of my father's influence: for example, Black (as before mentioned) and Fonblanque: most of these, however, we accounted only partial allies; Fonblanque, for instance, was always divergent from us on many important points. But indeed there was by no means complete unanimity among any portion of us, nor had any of us adopted implicitly all my father's opinions. For example, although his Essay on Government was regarded probably by all of us as a masterpiece of political wisdom, our adhesion by no means extended to the paragraph of it, in which he maintains that women may consistently with good government, be excluded from the suffrage, because their interest is the same with that of men. From this doctrine, I, and all those who formed my chosen associates, most positively dissented. It is due to my father to say that he denied having intended to affirm that women *should* be excluded, any more than men under the age of forty, concerning whom he maintained, in the very next paragraph, an exactly similar thesis. He was, as he truly said, not discussing whether the suffrage had better be restricted, but only (assuming that it is to be restricted) what is the utmost limit of restriction, which does not necessarily involve a sacrifice of the securities for good government. But I thought then, as I have always thought since, that the opinion which he acknowledged, no less than that which he disclaimed, is as great an error as any of those against which the Essay was directed; that the interest of women is included in that of men exactly as much and no more, as the interest of subjects is included in that of kings; and that every reason which exists for giving the suffrage to anybody, demands that it should not be withheld from women. This was also the general opinion of the younger proselytes; and it is pleasant to be able to say that Mr. Bentham, on this important point, was wholly on our side.

But though none of us, probably, agreed in every respect with my father, his opinions, as I said before, were the principal element which gave its colour and character to the little group of young men who were the first propagators of what was afterwards called " philosophic radicalism." Their mode of thinking was not characterized by Benthamism in any sense which has relation to Bentham as a chief or guide, but rather by a combination of Bentham's point of view with that of the modern political economy, and with the Hartleian metaphysics. Malthus's popula-

tion principle was quite as much a banner, and point of
union among us, as any opinion specially belonging to
Bentham. This great doctrine, originally brought forward
as an argument against the indefinite improvability of human
affairs, we took up with ardent zeal in the contrary sense,
as indicating the sole means of realizing that improvability
by securing full employment at high wages to the whole
labouring population through a voluntary restriction of
the increase of their numbers. The other leading characteristics of the creed, which we held in common with my
father, may be stated as follows:

In politics, an almost unbounded confidence in the
efficacy of two things: representative government, and complete freedom of discussion. So complete was my father's
reliance on the influence of reason over the minds of mankind, whenever it is allowed to reach them, that he felt
as if all would be gained if the whole population were
taught to read, if all sorts of opinions were allowed to be
addressed to them by word and in writing, and if by means
of the suffrage they could nominate a legislature to give
effect to the opinions they adopted. He thought that when
the legislature no longer represented a class interest, it
would aim at the general interest, honestly and with adequate wisdom; since the people would be sufficiently under
the guidance of educated intelligence, to make in general
a good choice of persons to represent them, and having done
so, to leave to those whom they had chosen a liberal dis-
cretion. Accordingly aristocratic rule, the government of
the Few in any of its shapes, being in his eyes the only
thing which stood between mankind and an administration
of their affairs by the best wisdom to be found among
them, was the object of his sternest disapprobation, and a
democratic suffrage the principal article of his political
creed, not on the ground of liberty, Rights of Man, or
any of the phrases, more or less significant, by which, up to
that time, democracy had usually been defended, but as

the most essential of " securities for good government."
In this, too, he held fast only to what he deemed essentials;
he was comparatively indifferent to monarchical or republican forms — far more so than Bentham, to whom a king,
in the character of " corrupter-general," appeared necessarily very noxious. Next to aristocracy, an established
church, or corporation of priests, as being by position the
great depravers of religion, and interested in opposing the
progress of the human mind, was the object of his greatest
detestation; though he disliked no clergyman personally
who did not deserve it, and was on terms of sincere friendship with several. In ethics, his moral feelings were energetic and rigid on all points which he deemed important to
human well being, while he was supremely indifferent in
opinion (though his indifference did not show itself in
personal conduct) to all those doctrines of the common
morality, which he thought had no foundation but in
asceticism and priestcraft. He looked forward, for example,
to a considerable increase of freedom in the relations
between the sexes, though without pretending to define
exactly what would be, or ought to be, the precise conditions
of that freedom. This opinion was connected in him with no
sensuality either of a theoretical or of a practical kind. He
anticipated, on the contrary, as one of the beneficial effects
of increased freedom, that the imagination would no longer
dwell upon the physical relation and its adjuncts, and swell
this into one of the principal objects of life; a perversion
of the imagination and feelings, which he regarded as one
of the deepest seated and most pervading evils in the human
mind. In psychology, his fundamental doctrine was the
formation of all human character by circumstances, through
the universal Principle of Association, and the consequent
unlimited possibility of improving the moral and intellectual condition of mankind by education. Of all his doctrines none was more important than this, or needs more to
be insisted on: unfortunately there is none which is more

contradictory to the prevailing tendencies of speculation, both in his time and since.

These various opinions were seized on with youthful fanaticism by the little knot of young men of whom I was one: and we put into them a sectarian spirit, from which, in intention at least, my father was wholly free. What we (or rather a phantom substituted in the place of us) were sometimes, by a ridiculous exaggeration, called by others, namely a " school," some of us for a time really hoped and aspired to be. The French *philosophes* of the eighteenth century were the example we sought to imitate, and we hoped to accomplish no less results. No one of the set went to so great excesses in this boyish ambition as I did; which might be shown by many particulars, were it not an useless waste of space and time.

All this, however, is properly only the outside of our existence; or, at least, the intellectual part alone, and no more than one side of that. In attempting to penetrate inward, and give any indication of what we were as human beings, I must be understood as speaking only of myself, of whom alone I can speak from sufficient knowledge; and I do not believe that the picture would suit any of my companions without many and great modifications.

I conceive that the description so often given of a Benthamite, as a mere reasoning machine, though extremely inapplicable to most of those who have been designated by that title, was during two or three years of my life not altogether untrue of me. It was perhaps as applicable to me as it can well be to any one just entering into life, to whom the common objects of desire must in general have at least the attraction of novelty. There is nothing very extraordinary in this fact: no youth of the age I then was, can be expected to be more than one thing, and this was the thing I happened to be. Ambition and desire of distinction, I had in abundance; and zeal for what I thought the good of mankind was my strongest sentiment, mixing with and colouring all others. But my zeal was as yet little else, at that period of my life, than zeal for speculative opinions. It had not its root in genuine benevolence, or sympathy with mankind; though these qualities held their due place in my ethical standard. Nor was it connected with any high enthusiasm for ideal nobleness. Yet of this feeling I was imaginatively very susceptible; but there was at that time an intermission of its natural aliment, poetical culture, while there was a superabundance of the discipline antagonistic to it, that of mere logic and analysis. Add to this that, as already mentioned, my father's teachings tended to the undervaluing of feeling. It was not that he was himself cold-hearted or insensible; I believe it was rather from the contrary quality; he thought that feeling could take care of itself; that there was sure to be enough of it if actions were properly cared about. Offended by the frequency with which, in ethical and philosophical controversy, feeling is made the ultimate reason and justification of conduct, instead of being itself called on for a justification, while, in practice, actions, the effect of which on human happiness is mischievous, are defended as being required by feeling, and the character of a person of feeling obtains a credit for desert, which he thought only due to actions, he had a real impatience of attributing praise to feeling, or of any but the most sparing reference to it, either in the estimation of persons or in the discussion of things. In addition to the influence which this characteristic in him had on me and others, we found all the opinions to which we attached most importance, constantly attacked on the ground of feeling. Utility was denounced as cold calculation; political economy as hard-hearted; anti-population doctrines as repulsive to the natural feelings of mankind. We retorted by the word "sentimentality," which, along with "declamation" and "vague generalities," served us as common terms of opprobrium. Although we were generally in the right, as against those who were opposed

to us, the effect was that the cultivation of feeling (except
the feelings of public and private duty), was not in much
esteem among us, and had very little place in the thoughts
of most of us, myself in particular. What we principally
thought of, was to alter people's opinions; to make them
believe according to evidence, and know what was their
real interest, which when they once knew, they would, we
thought, by the instrument of opinion, enforce a regard
to it upon one another. While fully recognizing the
superior excellence of unselfish benevolence and love of
justice, we did not expect the regeneration of mankind from
any direct action on those sentiments, but from the effect
of educated intellect, enlightening the selfish feelings.
Although this last is prodigiously important as a means of
improvement in the hands of those who are themselves
impelled by nobler principles of action, I do not believe
that any one of the survivors of the Benthamites or Utilitarians of that day, now relies mainly upon it for the
general amendment of human conduct.

From this neglect both in theory and in practice of the
cultivation of feeling, naturally resulted, among other
things, an undervaluing of poetry, and of Imagination
generally, as an element of human nature. It is, or was,
part of the popular notion of Benthamites, that they are
enemies of poetry: this was partly true of Bentham himself; he used to say that "all poetry is misrepresentation:"
but in the sense in which he said it, the same might have
been said of all impressive speech; of all representation
or inculcation more oratorical in its character than a sum
in arithmetic. An article of Bingham's in the first number
of the Westminster Review, in which he offered as an
explanation of something which he disliked in Moore, that
"Mr. Moore *is* a poet, and therefore is *not* a reasoner,"
did a good deal to attach the notion of hating poetry to
the writers in the Review. But the truth was that many
of us were great readers of poetry; Bingham himself had

been a writer of it, while as regards me (and the same thing might be said of my father), the correct statement would be, not that I disliked poetry, but that I was theoretically indifferent to it. I disliked any sentiments in poetry which I should have disliked in prose; and that included a great deal. And I was wholly blind to its place in human culture, as a means of educating the feelings. But I was always personally very susceptible to some kinds of it. In the most sectarian period of my Benthamism, I happened to look into Pope's Essay on Man, and though every opinion in it was contrary to mine, I well remember how powerfully it acted on my imagination. Perhaps at that time poetical composition of any higher type than eloquent discussion in verse, might not have produced a similar effect on me: at all events I seldom gave it an opportunity. This, however, was a mere passive state. Long before I had enlarged in any considerable degree, the basis of my intellectual creed, I had obtained in the natural course of my mental progress, poetic culture of the most valuable kind, by means of reverential admiration for the lives and characters of heroic persons; especially the heroes of philosophy. The same inspiring effect which so many of the benefactors of mankind have left on record that they had experienced from Plutarch's Lives, was produced on me by Plato's pictures of Socrates, and by some modern biographies, above all by Condorcet's Life of Turgot; a book well calculated to rouse the best sort of enthusiasm, since it contains one of the wisest and noblest of lives, delineated by one of the wisest and noblest of men. The heroic virtue of these glorious representatives of the opinions with which I sympathized, deeply affected me, and I perpetually recurred to them as others do to a favourite poet, when needing to be carried up into the more elevated regions of feeling and thought. I may observe by the way that this book cured me of my sectarian follies. The two or three pages beginning " Il regardait toute secte comme

nuisible," and explaining why Turgot always kept himself
perfectly distinct from the Encyclopedists, sank deeply
into my mind. I left off designating myself and others as
Utilitarians, and by the pronoun "we" or any other collective designation, I ceased to *afficher* sectarianism. My
real inward sectarianism I did not get rid of till later, and
much more gradually.

About the end of 1824, or beginning of 1825, Mr. Bentham, having lately got back his papers on Evidence from
M. Dumont (whose Traité des Preuves Judiciaires,
grounded on them, was then first completed and published)
resolved to have them printed in the original, and bethought
himself of me as capable of preparing them for the press;
in the same manner as his Book of Fallacies had been
recently edited by Bingham. I gladly undertook this task,
and it occupied nearly all my leisure for about a year,
exclusive of the time afterwards spent in seeing the five
large volumes through the press. Mr. Bentham had begun
this treatise three times, at considerable intervals, each time
in a different manner, and each time without reference to
the preceding: two of the three times he had gone over
nearly the whole subject. These three masses of manuscript it was my business to condense into a single treatise;
adopting the one last written as the groundwork, and incorporating with it as much of the two others as it had not
completely superseded. I had also to unroll such of Bentham's involved and parenthetical sentences, as seemed to
overpass by their complexity the measure of what readers
were likely to take the pains to understand. It was further
Mr. Bentham's particular desire that I should, from myself,
endeavour to supply any *lacunæ* which he had left; and at
his instance I read, for this purpose, the most authoritative
treatises on the English Law of Evidence, and commented
on a few of the objectionable points of the English rules,
which had escaped Bentham's notice. I also replied to the
objections which had been made to some of his doctrines by

reviewers of Dumont's book, and added a few supplementary remarks on some of the more abstract parts of the subject, such as the theory of improbability and impossibility. The controversial part of these editorial additions was written in a more assuming tone than became one so young and inexperienced as I was: but indeed I had never contemplated coming forward in my own person; and as an anonymous editor of Bentham, I fell into the tone of my author, not thinking it unsuitable to him or to the subject, however it might be so to me. My name as editor was put to the book after it was printed, at Mr. Bentham's positive desire, which I in vain attempted to persuade him to forego.

The time occupied in this editorial work was extremely well employed in respect to my own improvement. The " Rationale of Judicial Evidence " is one of the richest in matter of all Bentham's productions. The theory of evidence being in itself one of the most important of his subjects, and ramifying into most of the others, the book contains, very fully developed, a great proportion of all his best thoughts: while, among more special things, it comprises the most elaborate exposure of the vices and defects of English law, as it then was, which is to be found in his works; not confined to the law of evidence, but including, by way of illustrative episode, the entire procedure or practice of Westminster Hall. The direct knowledge, therefore, which I obtained from the book, and which was imprinted upon me much more thoroughly than it could have been by mere reading, was itself no small acquisition. But this occupation did for me what might seem less to be expected; it gave a great start to my powers of composition. Everything which I wrote subsequently to this editorial employment, was markedly superior to anything that I had written before it. Bentham's later style, as the world knows, was heavy and cumbersome, from the excess of a good quality, the love of precision, which made him introduce clause within clause into the heart of every sentence, that the reader might receive into his mind all the modifications and qualifications simultaneously with the main proposition: and the habit grew on him until his sentences became, to those not accustomed to them, most laborious reading. But his earlier style, that of the Fragment on Government, Plan of a Judicial Establishment, &c., is a model of liveliness and ease combined with fulness of matter, scarcely ever surpassed: and of this earlier style there were many striking specimens in the manuscripts on Evidence, all of which I endeavoured to preserve. So long a course of this admirable writing had a considerable effect upon my own; and I added to it by the assiduous reading of other writers, both French and English, who combined, in a remarkable degree, ease with force, such as Goldsmith, Fielding, Pascal, Voltaire, and Courier. Through these influences my writing lost the jejuneness of my early compositions; the bones and cartilages began to clothe themselves with flesh, and the style became, at times, lively and almost light.

This improvement was first exhibited in a new field. Mr. Marshall, of Leeds, father of the present generation of Marshalls, the same who was brought into Parliament for Yorkshire, when the representation forfeited by Grampound was transferred to it, an earnest parliamentary reformer, and a man of large fortune, of which he made a liberal use, had been much struck with Bentham's Book of Fallacies: and the thought had occurred to him that it would be useful to publish annually the Parliamentary Debates, not in the chronological order of Hansard, but classified according to subjects, and accompanied by a commentary pointing out the fallacies of the speakers. With this intention, he very naturally addressed himself to the editor of the Book of Fallacies; and Bingham, with the assistance of Charles Austin, undertook the editorship. The work was called " Parliamentary History and Review." Its sale was not sufficient to keep it in existence, and it only lasted three years. It excited, however, some attention among parliamentary and political people. The best strength of the party was put forth in it; and its execution did them much more credit than that of the Westminster Review had ever done. Bingham and Charles Austin wrote much in it; as did Strutt, Romilly, and several other liberal lawyers. My father wrote one article in his best style; the elder Austin another. Coulson wrote one of great merit. It fell to my lot to lead off the first number by an article on the principal topic of the session (that of 1825), the Catholic Association and the Catholic disabilities. In the second number I wrote an elaborate Essay on the commercial crisis of 1825 and the Currency Debates. In the third I had two articles, one on a minor subject, the other on the Reciprocity principle in commerce, *à propos* of a celebrated diplomatic correspondence between Canning and Gallatin. These writings were no longer mere reproductions and applications of the doctrines I had been taught; they were original thinking, as far as that name can be applied to old ideas in new forms and connexions: and I do not exceed the truth in saying that there was a maturity, and a well-digested character about them, which there had not been in any of my previous performances. In execution, therefore, they were not at all juvenile; but their subjects have either gone by, or have been so much better treated since, that they are entirely superseded, and should remain buried in the same oblivion with my contributions to the first dynasty of the Westminster Review.

While thus engaged in writing for the public, I did not neglect other modes of self-cultivation. It was at this time that I learnt German; beginning it on the Hamiltonian method, for which purpose I and several of my companions formed a class. For several years from this period, our social studies assumed a shape which contributed very much to my mental progress. The idea occurred to

us of carrying on, by reading and conversation, a joint
study of several of the branches of science which we wished
to be masters of. We assembled to the number of a dozen
or more. Mr. Grote lent a room of his house in Thread-
needle Street for the purpose, and his partner, Prescott,
one of the three original members of the Utilitarian Society,
made one among us. We met two mornings in every
week, from half-past eight till ten, at which hour most of
us were called off to our daily occupations. Our first subject was Political Economy. We chose some systematic
treatise as our text-book; my father's " Elements " being
our first choice. One of us read aloud a chapter, or some
smaller portion of the book. The discussion was then
opened, and any one who had an objection, or other remark
to make, made it. Our rule was to discuss thoroughly
every point raised, whether great or small, prolonging the
discussion until all who took part were satisfied with the
conclusion they had individually arrived at; and to follow
up every topic of collateral speculation which the chapter
or the conversation suggested, never leaving it until we
had untied every knot which we found. We repeatedly
kept up the discussion of some one point for several weeks,
thinking intently on it during the intervals of our meetings,
and contriving solutions of the new difficulties which had
risen up in the last morning's discussion. When we had
finished in this way my father's Elements, we went in the
same manner through Ricardo's Principles of Political
Economy, and Bailey's Dissertation on Value. These close
and vigorous discussions were not only improving in a high
degree to those who took part in them, but brought out
new views of some topics of abstract Political Economy.
The theory of International Values which I afterwards
published, emanated from these conversations, as did also
the modified form of Ricardo's theory of Profits, laid down
in my Essay on Profits and Interest. Those among us with
whom new speculations chiefly originated, were Ellis,

Graham, and I; though others gave valuable aid to the discussions, especially Prescott and Roebuck, the one by his knowledge, the other by his dialectical acuteness. The theories of International Values and of Profits were excogitated and worked out in about equal proportions by myself and Graham: and if our original project had been executed, my "Essays on some Unsettled Questions of Political Economy" would have been brought out along with some papers of his, under our joint names. But when my exposition came to be written, I found that I had so much over-estimated my agreement with him, and he dissented so much from the most original of the two Essays, that on International Values, that I was obliged to consider the theory as now exclusively mine, and it came out as such when published many years later. I may mention that among the alterations which my father made in revising his Elements for the third edition, several were founded on criticisms elicited by these conversations; and in particular he modified his opinions (though not to the extent of our new speculations) on both the points to which I have adverted.

When we had enough of political economy, we took up the syllogistic logic in the same manner, Grote now joining us. Our first text-book was Aldrich, but being disgusted with its superficiality, we reprinted one of the most finished among the many manuals of the school logic, which my father, a great collector of such books, possessed, the Manuductio ad Logicam of the Jesuit Du Trieu. After finishing this, we took up Whately's Logic, then first republished from the Encyclopædia Metropolitana, and finally the " Computatio sive Logica " of Hobbes. These books, dealt with in our manner, afforded a wide range for original metaphysical speculation: and most of what has been done in the First Book of my System of Logic, to rationalize and correct the principles and distinctions of the school logicians, and to improve the theory of the Import of

Propositions, had its origin in these discussions; Graham
and I originating most of the novelties, while Grote and
others furnished an excellent tribunal or test.   From this
time I formed the project of writing a book on Logic,
though on a much humbler scale than the one I ultimately
executed.

Having done with Logic, we launched into analytic
psychology, and having chosen Hartley for our text-book,
we raised Priestley's edition to an extravagant price by
searching through London to furnish each of us with a
copy.   When we had finished Hartley, we suspended our
meetings; but my father's Analysis of the Mind being published soon after, we reassembled for the purpose of reading it.   With this our exercises ended.   I have always
dated from these conversations my own real inauguration
as an original and independent thinker.   It was also
through them that I acquired, or very much strengthened,
a mental habit to which I attribute all that I have ever
done, or ever shall do, in speculation; that of never accepting half-solutions of difficulties as complete; never aban-
doning a puzzle, but again and again returning to it until
it was cleared up; never allowing obscure corners of a subject to remain unexplored, because they did not appear important; never thinking that I perfectly understood any
part of a subject until I understood the whole.

Our doings from 1825 to 1830 in the way of public
speaking, filled a considerable place in my life during those
years, and as they had important effects on my development, something ought to be said of them.

There was for some time in existence a society of
Owenites, called the Co-operative Society, which met for
weekly public discussions in Chancery Lane.   In the early
part of 1825, accident brought Roebuck in contact with
several of its members, and led to his attending one or
two of the meetings and taking part in the debate in opposition to Owenism.   Some one of us started the notion

of going there in a body and having a general battle: and Charles Austin and some of his friends who did not usually take part in our joint exercises, entered into the project. It was carried out by concert with the principal members of the Society, themselves nothing loth, as they naturally preferred a controversy with opponents to a tame discussion among their own body. The question of population was proposed as the subject of debate: Charles Austin led the case on our side with a brilliant speech, and the fight was kept up by adjournment through five or six weekly meetings before crowded auditories, including along with the members of the Society and their friends, many hearers and some speakers from the Inns of Court. When this debate was ended, another was commenced on the general merits of Owen's system: and the contest altogether lasted about three months. It was a *lutte corps-à-corps* between Owenites and political economists, whom the Owenites regarded as their most inveterate opponents: but it was a perfectly friendly dispute. We who represented political economy, had the same objects in view as they had, and took pains to show it; and the principal champion on their side was a very estimable man, with whom I was well acquainted, Mr. William Thompson, of Cork, author of a book on the Distribution of Wealth, and of an " Appeal " in behalf of women against the passage relating to them in my father's Essay on Government. Ellis, Roebuck, and I took an active part in the debate, and among those from the Inns of Court who joined in it, I remember Charles Villiers. The other side obtained also, on the population question, very efficient support from without. The well-known Gale Jones, then an elderly man, made one of his florid speeches; but the speaker with whom I was most struck, though I dissented from nearly every word he said, was Thirlwall, the historian, since Bishop of St. David's, then a Chancery barrister, unknown except by a high reputation for eloquence acquired at the Cambridge

Union before the era of Austin and Macaulay. His speech was in answer to one of mine. Before he had uttered ten sentences, I set him down as the best speaker I had ever heard, and I have never since heard any one whom I placed above him.

The great interest of these debates predisposed some of those who took part in them, to catch at a suggestion thrown out by McCulloch, the political economist, that a society was wanted in London similar to the Speculative Society at Edinburgh, in which Brougham, Horner, and others first cultivated public speaking. Our experience at the Co-operative Society seemed to give cause for being sanguine as to the sort of men who might be brought together in London for such a purpose. McCulloch mentioned the matter to several young men of influence, to whom he was then giving private lessons in political economy. Some of these entered warmly into the project, particularly George Villiers, afterwards Earl of Clarendon. He and his brothers, Hyde and Charles, Romilly, Charles Austin and I, with some others, met and agreed on a plan. We determined to meet once a fortnight from November to June, at the Freemasons' Tavern, and we had soon a splendid list of members, containing, along with several members of parliament, nearly all the most noted speakers of the Cambridge Union and of the Oxford United Debating Society. It is curiously illustrative of the tendencies of the time, that our principal difficulty in recruiting for the Society was to find a sufficient number of Tory speakers. Almost all whom we could press into the service were Liberals, of different orders and degrees. Besides those already named, we had Macaulay, Thirlwall, Praed, Lord Howick, Samuel Wilberforce (afterwards Bishop of Oxford), Charles Poulett Thomson (afterwards Lord Sydenham), Edward and Henry Lytton Bulwer, Fonblanque, and many others whom I cannot now recollect, but who made themselves afterwards more or less conspicuous in public or literary life. Nothing could seem more promising. But when the time for action drew near, and it was necessary to fix on a President, and find somebody to open the first debate, none of our celebrities would consent to perform either office. Of the many who were pressed on the subject, the only one who could be prevailed on was a man of whom I knew very little, but who had taken high honours at Oxford and was said to have acquired a great oratorical reputation there; who some time afterwards became a Tory member of parliament. He accordingly was fixed on, both for filling the President's chair and for making the first speech. The important day arrived; the benches were crowded; all our great speakers were present, to judge of, but not to help our efforts. The Oxford orator's speech was a complete failure. This threw a damp on the whole concern: the speakers who followed were few, and none of them did their best: the affair was a complete *fiasco;* and the oratorical celebrities we had counted on went away never to return, giving to me at least a lesson in knowledge of the world. This unexpected breakdown altered my whole relation to the project. I had not anticipated taking a prominent part, or speaking much or often, particularly at first, but I now saw that the success of the scheme depended on the new men, and I put my shoulder to the wheel. I opened the second question, and from that time spoke in nearly every debate. It was very uphill work for some time. The three Villiers' and Romilly stuck to us for some time longer, but the patience of all the founders of the Society was at last exhausted, except me and Roebuck. In the season following, 1826–7, things began to mend. We had acquired two excellent Tory speakers, Hayward and Shee (afterwards Sergeant Shee): the radical side was reinforced by Charles Buller, Cockburn, and others of the second generation of Cambridge Benthamites; and with their and other occasional aid, and the two Tories as well as Roebuck and me for regular speakers, almost every debate was a

bataille rangée between the "philosophic radicals" and the
Tory lawyers; until our conflicts were talked about, and
several persons of note and consideration came to hear us.
This happened still more in the subsequent seasons, 1828
and 1829, when the Coleridgians, in the persons of Maurice
and Sterling, made their appearance in the Society as a
second Liberal and even Radical party, on totally different
grounds from Benthamism and vehemently opposed to it;
bringing into these discussions the general doctrines and
modes of thought of the European reaction against the philosophy of the eighteenth century; and adding a third and
very important belligerent party to our contests, which were
now no bad exponent of the movement of opinion among
the most cultivated part of the new generation. Our debates were very different from those of common debating
societies, for they habitually consisted of the strongest arguments and most philosophic principles which either side was
able to produce, thrown often into close and *serré* confuta-
tions of one another. The practice was necessarily very
useful to us, and eminently so to me. I never, indeed,
acquired real fluency, and had always a bad and ungraceful
delivery; but I could make myself listened to: and as I
always wrote my speeches when, from the feelings involved,
or the nature of the ideas to be developed, expression seemed
important, I greatly increased my power of effective writing; acquiring not only an ear for smoothness and rhythm,
but a practical sense for *telling* sentences, and an immediate
criterion of their telling property, by their effect on a mixed
audience.

The Society, and the preparation for it, together with the
preparation for the morning conversations which were going
on simultaneously, occupied the greater part of my leisure;
and made me feel it a relief when, in the spring of 1828,
I ceased to write for the Westminster. The Review had
fallen into difficulties. Though the sale of the first number
had been very encouraging, the permanent sale had never,

I believe, been sufficient to pay the expenses, on the scale on which the review was carried on. Those expenses had been considerably, but not sufficiently, reduced. One of the editors, Southern, had resigned; and several of the writers, including my father and me, who had been paid like other contributors for our earlier articles, had latterly written without payment. Nevertheless, the original funds were nearly or quite exhausted, and if the Review was to be continued some new arrangement of its affairs had become indispensable. My father and I had several conferences with Bowring on the subject. We were willing to do our utmost for maintaining the Review as an organ of our opinions, but not under Bowring's editorship: while the impossibility of its any longer supporting a paid editor, afforded a ground on which, without affront to him, we could propose to dispense with his services. We and some of our friends were prepared to carry on the Review as unpaid writers, either finding among ourselves an unpaid editor, or sharing the editorship among us. But while this negotiation was proceeding with Bowring's apparent acquiescence, he was carrying on another in a different quarter (with Colonel Perronet Thompson), of which we received the first intimation in a letter from Bowring as editor, informing us merely that an arrangement had been made, and proposing to us to write for the next number, with promise of payment. We did not dispute Bowring's right to bring about, if he could, an arrangement more favourable to himself than the one we had proposed; but we thought the concealment which he had practised towards us, while seemingly entering into our own project, an affront: and even had we not thought so, we were indisposed to expend any more of our time and trouble in attempting to write up the Review under his management. Accordingly my father excused himself from writing; though two or three years later, on great pressure, he did write one more political article. As for me, I positively refused. And thus ended my connexion

with the original Westminster. The last article which I
wrote in it had cost me more labour than any previous; but
it was a labour of love, being a defence of the early French
Revolutionists against the Tory misrepresentations of Sir
Walter Scott, in the introduction to his Life of Napoleon.
The number of books which I read for this purpose, making
notes and extracts — even the number I had to buy (for
in those days there was no public or subscription library
from which books of reference could be taken home), far
exceeded the worth of the immediate object; but I had at
that time a half-formed intention of writing a History of
the French Revolution; and though I never executed it, my
collections afterwards were very useful to Carlyle for a
similar purpose.

Chapter V

A CRISIS IN MY MENTAL HISTORY. ONE STAGE ONWARD.

FOR some years after this I wrote very little, and nothing regularly, for publication: and great were the advantages which I derived from the intermission. It was of no common importance to me, at this period, to be able to digest and mature my thoughts for my own mind only, without any immediate call for giving them out in print. Had I gone on writing, it would have much disturbed the important transformation in my opinions and character, which took place during those years. The origin of this transformation, or at least the process by which I was prepared for it, can only be explained by turning some distance back.

From the winter of 1821, when I first read Bentham, and especially from the commencement of the Westminster Review, I had what might truly be called an object in life; to be a reformer of the world. My conception of my own happiness was entirely identified with this object. The personal sympathies I wished for were those of fellow labourers in this enterprise. I endeavoured to pick up as many flowers as I could by the way; but as a serious and permanent personal satisfaction to rest upon, my whole reliance was placed on this; and I was accustomed to felicitate myself on the certainty of a happy life which I enjoyed, through placing my happiness in something durable and distant, in which some progress might be always making, while it could never be exhausted by complete attainment. This did very well for several years, during which the general improvement going on in the world and the idea of myself as engaged with others in struggling to promote it, seemed enough to fill up an interesting and animated existence. But the time came when I awakened from this as from a dream. It was in the autumn of 1826. I was in a dull state of nerves, such as everybody is occasionally liable to; unsusceptible to enjoyment or pleasurable excitement; one of those moods when what is pleasure at other times, becomes insipid or indifferent; the state, I should think, in which converts to Methodism usually are, when smitten by their first "conviction of sin." In this frame of mind it occurred to me to put the question directly to myself: "Suppose that all your objects in life were realized; that all the changes in institutions and opinions which you are looking forward to, could be completely effected at this very instant: would this be a great joy and happiness to you?" And an irrepressible self-consciousness distinctly answered, "No!" At this my heart sank within me: the whole foundation on which my life was constructed fell down. All my happiness was to have been found in the continual pursuit of this end. The end had ceased to charm, and how could there ever again be any interest in the means? I seemed to have nothing left to live for.

At first I hoped that the cloud would pass away of itself; but it did not. A night's sleep, the sovereign remedy for the smaller vexations of life, had no effect on it. I awoke to a renewed consciousness of the woful fact. I carried it with me into all companies, into all occupations. Hardly anything had power to cause me even a few minutes oblivion of it. For some months the cloud seemed to grow thicker and thicker. The lines in Coleridge's "Dejection" — I was not then acquainted with them — exactly describe my case:

> "A grief without a pang, void, dark and drear,
>   A drowsy, stifled, unimpassioned grief,
>   Which finds no natural outlet or relief
>   In word, or sigh, or tear."

In vain I sought relief from my favourite books; those memorials of past nobleness and greatness from which I had always hitherto drawn strength and animation. I read them now without feeling, or with the accustomed feeling *minus* all its charm; and I became persuaded, that my love of mankind, and of excellence for its own sake, had worn itself out. I sought no comfort by speaking to others of what I felt. If I had loved any one sufficiently to make confiding my griefs a necessity, I should not have been in the condition I was. I felt, too, that mine was not an interesting, or in any way respectable distress. There was nothing in it to attract sympathy. Advice, if I had known where to seek it, would have been most precious. The words of Macbeth to the physician often occurred to my thoughts. But there was no one on whom I could build the faintest hope of such assistance. My father, to whom it would have been natural to me to have recourse in any practical difficulties, was the last person to whom, in such a case as this, I looked for help. Everything convinced me that he had no knowledge of any such mental state as I was suffering from, and that even if he could be made to understand it, he was not the physician who could heal it. My education, which was wholly his work, had been conducted without any regard to the possibility of its ending in this result; and I saw no use in giving him the pain of thinking that his plans had failed, when the failure was probably irremediable, and, at all events, beyond the power of *his* remedies. Of other friends, I had at that time none to whom I had any hope of making my condition intelligible. It was however abundantly intelligible to myself; and the more I dwelt upon it, the more hopeless it appeared.

My course of study had led me to believe, that all mental and moral feelings and qualities, whether of a good or of a bad kind, were the results of association; that we love one thing, and hate another, take pleasure in one sort of action or contemplation, and pain in another sort, through the clinging of pleasurable or painful ideas to those things, from the effect of education or of experience. As a corollary from this, I had always heard it maintained by my father, and was myself convinced, that the object of education should be to form the strongest possible associations of the salutary class; associations of pleasure with all things beneficial to the great whole, and of pain with all things hurtful to it. This doctrine appeared inexpugnable; but it now seemed to me, on retrospect, that my teachers had occupied themselves but superficially with the means of forming and keeping up these salutary associations. They seemed to have trusted altogether to the old familiar instruments, praise and blame, reward and punishment. Now, I did not doubt that by these means, begun early, and applied unremittingly, intense associations of pain and pleasure, especially of pain, might be created, and might produce desires and aversions capable of lasting undiminished to the end of life. But there must always be something artificial and casual in associations thus produced. The pains and pleasures thus forcibly associated with things, are not connected with them by any natural tie; and it is therefore, I thought, essential to the durability of these associations, that they should have become so intense and inveterate as to be practically indissoluble, before the habitual exercise of the power of analysis had commenced. For I now saw, or thought I saw, what I had always before received with incredulity — that the habit of analysis has a tendency to wear away the feelings: as indeed it has, when no other mental habit is cultivated, and the analysing spirit remains without its natural complements and correctives. The very excellence of analysis (I argued) is that it tends to weaken and undermine whatever is the result of prejudice; that it enables us mentally to separate ideas which have only casually clung together: and no associations whatever could ultimately resist this dissolving force, were it not that we owe to analysis our clearest knowledge of the permanent sequences in nature; the real connexions between Things, not dependent on our will and feelings; natural laws, by virtue of which, in many cases, one thing is inseparable from another in fact; which laws, in proportion as they are clearly perceived and imaginatively realized, cause our ideas of things which are always joined together in Nature, to cohere more and more closely in our thoughts. Analytic habits may thus even strengthen the associations between causes and effects, means and ends, but tend altogether to weaken those which are, to speak familiarly, a *mere* matter of feeling. They are therefore (I thought) favourable to prudence and clear-sightedness, but a perpetual worm at the root both of the passions and of the virtues; and, above all, fearfully undermine all desires, and all pleasures, which are the effects of association, that is, according to the theory I held, all except the purely physical and organic; of the entire insufficiency of which to make life desirable, no one had a stronger conviction than I had. These were the laws of human nature, by which, as it seemed to me, I had been brought to my present state. All those to whom I looked up, were of opinion that the pleasure of sympathy with human beings, and the feelings which made the good of others, and especially of mankind on a large scale, the object of existence, were the greatest and surest sources of happiness. Of the truth of this I was convinced, but to know that a feeling would make me happy if I had it, did not give me the feeling. My education, I thought, had failed to create these feelings in sufficient strength to resist the dissolving influence of analysis, while the whole course of my intellectual cultivation had made precocious and premature analysis the inveterate habit of my mind. I was thus, as I said to myself, left stranded at the commencement of my voyage, with a well-equipped ship and a rudder, but no sail; without any real desire for the ends which I had been

so carefully fitted out to work for: no delight in virtue,
or the general good, but also just as little in anything else.
The fountains of vanity and ambition seemed to have dried
up within me, as completely as those of benevolence. I
had had (as I reflected) some gratification of vanity at too
early an age: I had obtained some distinction, and felt myself of some importance, before the desire of distinction
and of importance had grown into a passion: and little as
it was which I had attained, yet having been attained too
early, like all pleasures enjoyed too soon, it had made me
blasé and indifferent to the pursuit. Thus neither selfish
nor unselfish pleasures were pleasures to me. And there
seemed no power in nature sufficient to begin the formation
of my character anew, and create in a mind now irretriev-
ably analytic, fresh associations of pleasure with any of the
objects of human desire.

These were the thoughts which mingled with the dry
heavy dejection of the melancholy winter of 1826–7.
During this time I was not incapable of my usual occupations. I went on with them mechanically, by the mere
force of habit. I had been so drilled in a certain sort of
mental exercise, that I could still carry it on when all the
spirit had gone out of it. I even composed and spoke
several speeches at the debating society, how, or with what
degree of success, I know not. Of four years continual
speaking at that society, this is the only year of which I
remember next to nothing. Two lines of Coleridge, in
whom alone of all writers I have found a true description
of what I felt, were often in my thoughts, not at this time
(for I had never read them), but in a later period of the
same mental malady:

> "Work without hope draws nectar in a sieve,
> And hope without an object cannot live."

In all probability my case was by no means so peculiar as
I fancied it, and I doubt not that many others have passed

I had now learnt by experience that the passive susceptibilities needed to be cultivated as well as the active capacities, and required to be nourished and enriched as well as
guided. I did not, for an instant, lose sight of, or under-
value, that part of the truth which I had seen before; I
never turned recreant to intellectual culture, or ceased to
consider the power and practice of analysis as an essential
condition both of individual and of social improvement.
But I thought that it had consequences which required to
be corrected, by joining other kinds of cultivation with it.
The maintenance of a due balance among the faculties, now
seemed to me of primary importance. The cultivation of
the feelings became one of the cardinal points in my ethical
and philosophical creed. And my thoughts and inclina-
tions turned in an increasing degree towards whatever
seemed capable of being instrumental to that object.

I now began to find meaning in the things which I had
read or heard about the importance of poetry and art as
instruments of human culture. But it was some time
longer before I began to know this by personal experience.
The only one of the imaginative arts in which I had from
childhood taken great pleasure, was music; the best effect
of which (and in this it surpasses perhaps every other art)
consists in exciting enthusiasm; in winding up to a high
pitch those feelings of an elevated kind which are already
in the character, but to which this excitement gives a glow
and a fervour, which, though transitory at its utmost height,
is precious for sustaining them at other times. This effect
of music I had often experienced; but like all my pleasurable
susceptibilities it was suspended during the gloomy period.
I had sought relief again and again from this quarter, but
found none. After the tide had turned, and I was in
process of recovery, I had been helped forward by music,
but in a much less elevated manner. I at this time first
became acquainted with Weber's Oberon, and the extreme
pleasure which I drew from its delicious melodies did me

good, by showing me a source of pleasure to which I was as susceptible as ever. The good, however, was much impaired by the thought, that the pleasure of music (as is quite true of such pleasure as this was, that of mere tune) fades with familiarity, and requires either to be revived by intermittence, or fed by continual novelty. And it is very characteristic both of my then state, and of the general tone of my mind at this period of my life, that I was seriously tormented by the thought of the exhaustibility of musical combinations. The octave consists only of five tones and two semi-tones, which can be put together in only a limited number of ways, of which but a small proportion are beautiful: most of these, it seemed to me, must have been already discovered, and there could not be room for a long succession of Mozarts and Webers, to strike out, as these had done, entirely new and surpassingly rich veins of musical beauty. This source of anxiety may, perhaps, be thought to resemble that of the philosophers of Laputa, who feared lest the sun should be burnt out. It was, however, connected with the best feature in my character, and the only good point to be found in my very unromantic and in no way honourable distress. For though my dejection, honestly looked at, could not be called other than egotistical, produced by the ruin, as I thought, of my fabric of happiness, yet the destiny of mankind in general was ever in my thoughts, and could not be separated from my own. I felt that the flaw in my life, must be a flaw in life itself; that the question was, whether, if the reformers of society and government could succeed in their objects, and every person in the community were free and in a state of physical comfort, the pleasures of life, being no longer kept up by struggle and privation, would cease to be pleasures. And I felt that unless I could see my way to some better hope than this for human happiness in general, my dejection must continue; but that if I could see such an outlet, I should then look on the world with pleasure;

content as far as I was myself concerned, with any fair share of the general lot.

This state of my thoughts and feelings made the fact of my reading Wordsworth for the first time (in the autumn of 1828), an important event in my life. I took up the collection of his poems from curiosity, with no expectation of mental relief from it, though I had before resorted to poetry with that hope. In the worst period of my depression, I had read through the whole of Byron (then new to me), to try whether a poet, whose peculiar department was supposed to be that of the intenser feelings, could rouse any feeling in me. As might be expected, I got no good from this reading, but the reverse. The poet's state of mind was too like my own. His was the lament of a man who had worn out all pleasures, and who seemed to think that life, to all who possess the good things of it, must necessarily be the vapid, uninteresting thing which I found it. His Harold and Manfred had the same burthen on them which I had; and I was not in a frame of mind to derive any comfort from the vehement sensual passion of his Giaours, or the sullenness of his Laras. But while Byron was exactly what did not suit my condition, Wordsworth was exactly what did. I had looked into the Excursion two or three years before, and found little in it; and I should probably have found as little, had I read it at this time. But the miscellaneous poems, in the two-volume edition of 1815 (to which little of value was added in the latter part of the author's life), proved to be the precise thing for my mental wants at that particular juncture.

In the first place, these poems addressed themselves powerfully to one of the strongest of my pleasurable susceptibilities, the love of rural objects and natural scenery; to which I had been indebted not only for much of the pleasure of my life, but quite recently for relief from one of my longest relapses into depression. In this power of rural beauty over me, there was a foundation laid for taking

pleasure in Wordsworth's poetry; the more so, as his
scenery lies mostly among mountains, which, owing to my
early Pyrenean excursion, were my ideal of natural
beauty. But Wordsworth would never have had any
great effect on me, if he had merely placed before me
beautiful pictures of natural scenery. Scott does this
still better than Wordsworth, and a very second-rate
landscape does it more effectually than any poet. What
made Wordsworth's poems a medicine for my state of
mind, was that they expressed, not mere outward beauty,
but states of feeling, and of thought coloured by feeling,
under the excitement of beauty. They seemed to be the
very culture of the feelings, which I was in quest of. In
them I seemed to draw from a source of inward joy, of
sympathetic and imaginative pleasure, which could be
shared in by all human beings; which had no connexion
with struggle or imperfection, but would be made richer
by every improvement in the physical or social condition
of mankind. From them I seemed to learn what would
be the perennial sources of happiness, when all the greater
evils of life shall have been removed. And I felt myself
at once better and happier as I came under their influence.
There have certainly been, even in our own age, greater
poets than Wordsworth; but poetry of deeper and loftier
feeling could not have done for me at that time what his
did. I needed to be made to feel that there was real, permanent happiness in tranquil contemplation. Wordsworth
taught me this, not only without turning away from, but
with a greatly increased interest in the common feelings
and common destiny of human beings. And the delight
which these poems gave me, proved that with culture of
this sort, there was nothing to dread from the most confirmed habit of analysis. At the conclusion of the Poems
came the famous Ode, falsely called Platonic, " Intimations
of Immortality: " in which, along with more than his usual
sweetness of melody and rhythm, and along with the two

passages of grand imagery but bad philosophy so often quoted, I found that he too had had similar experience to mine; that he also had felt that the first freshness of youthful enjoyment of life was not lasting; but that he had sought for compensation, and found it, in the way in which he was now teaching me to find it. The result was that I gradually, but completely, emerged from my habitual depression, and was never again subject to it. I long continued to value Wordsworth less according to his intrinsic merits, than by the measure of what he had done for me. Compared with the greatest poets, he may be said to be the poet of unpoetical natures, possessed of quiet and contemplative tastes. But unpoetical natures are precisely those which require poetic cultivation. This cultivation Wordsworth is much more fitted to give, than poets who are intrinsically far more poets than he.

It so fell out that the merits of Wordsworth were the occasion of my first public declaration of my new way of thinking, and separation from those of my habitual companions who had not undergone a similar change. The person with whom at that time I was most in the habit of comparing notes on such subjects was Roebuck, and I induced him to read Wordsworth, in whom he also at first seemed to find much to admire: but I, like most Wordsworthians, threw myself into strong antagonism to Byron, both as a poet and as to his influence on the character. Roebuck, all whose instincts were those of action and struggle, had, on the contrary, a strong relish and great admiration of Byron, whose writings he regarded as the poetry of human life, while Wordsworth's, according to him, was that of flowers and butterflies. We agreed to have the fight out at our Debating Society, where we accordingly discussed for two evenings the comparative merits of Byron and Wordsworth, propounding and illustrating by long recitations our respective theories of poetry: Sterling also, in a brilliant speech, putting forward his par-

ticular theory.   This was the first debate on any weighty
subject in which Roebuck and I had been on opposite sides.
The schism between us widened from this time more and
more, though we continued for some years longer to be
companions.   In the beginning, our chief divergence
related to the cultivation of the feelings.   Roebuck was in
many respects very different from the vulgar notion of a
Benthamite or Utilitarian.   He was a lover of poetry and
of most of the fine arts.   He took great pleasure in music,
in dramatic performances, especially in painting, and himself drew and designed landscapes with great facility and
beauty.   But he never could be made to see that these
things have any value as aids in the formation of character.   Personally, instead of being, as Benthamites are supposed to be, void of feeling, he had very quick and strong
sensibilities.   But, like most Englishmen who have feelings,
he found his feelings stand very much in his way.   He
was much more susceptible to the painful sympathies than
to the pleasurable, and looking for his happiness elsewhere,
he wished that his feelings should be deadened rather than
quickened.   And, in truth, the English character, and English social circumstances, make it so seldom possible to
derive happiness from the exercise of the sympathies, that
it is not wonderful if they count for little in an Englishman's scheme of life.   In most other countries the para-
mount importance of the sympathies as a constituent of
individual happiness is an axiom, taken for granted rather
than needing any formal statement; but most English
thinkers almost seem to regard them as necessary evils,
required for keeping men's actions benevolent and com-
passionate.   Roebuck was, or appeared to be, this kind of
Englishman.   He saw little good in any cultivation of the
feelings, and none at all in cultivating them through the
imagination, which he thought was only cultivating illusions.
It was in vain I urged on him that the imaginative emotion
which an idea, when vividly conceived, excites in us, is not

an illusion but a fact, as real as any of the other qualities of objects; and far from implying anything erroneous and delusive in our mental apprehension of the object, is quite consistent with the most accurate knowledge and most perfect practical recognition of all its physical and intellectual laws and relations. The intensest feeling of the beauty of a cloud lighted by the setting sun, is no hindrance to my knowing that the cloud is vapour of water, subject to all the laws of vapours in a state of suspension; and I am just as likely to allow for, and act on, these physical laws whenever there is occasion to do so, as if I had been incapable of perceiving any distinction between beauty and ugliness.

While my intimacy with Roebuck diminished, I fell more and more into friendly intercourse with our Coleridgian adversaries in the Society, Frederick Maurice and John Sterling, both subsequently so well known, the former by his writings, the latter through the biographies by Hare and Carlyle. Of these two friends, Maurice was the thinker, Sterling the orator, and impassioned expositor of thoughts which, at this period, were almost entirely formed for him by Maurice. With Maurice I had for some time been acquainted through Eyton Tooke, who had known him at Cambridge, and though my discussions with him were almost always disputes, I had carried away from them much that helped to build up my new fabric of thought, in the same way as I was deriving much from Coleridge, and from the writings of Goethe and other German authors which I read during those years. I have so deep a respect for Maurice's character and purposes, as well as for his great mental gifts, that it is with some unwillingness I say anything which may seem to place him on a less high eminence than I would gladly be able to accord to him. But I have always thought that there was more intellectual power wasted in Maurice than in any other of my contemporaries. Few of them certainly have had so much to waste. Great powers of generalization, rare ingenuity and subtlety, and a wide perception of important and unobvious truths, served him not for putting something better into the place of the worthless heap of received opinions on the great subjects of thought, but for proving to his own mind that the Church of England had known everything from the first, and that all the truths on the ground of which the Church and orthodoxy have been attacked (many of which he saw as clearly as any one) are not only consistent with the Thirty-nine articles, but are better understood and expressed in those articles than by any one who rejects them.   I have never been able to find any other explanation of this, than by attributing it to that timidity of conscience, combined with original sensitiveness of temperament, which has so often driven highly gifted men into Romanism from the need of a firmer support than they can find in the independent conclusions of their own judgment.   Any more vulgar kind of timidity no one who knew Maurice would ever think of imputing to him, even if he had not given public proof of his freedom from it, by his ultimate collision with some of the opinions commonly regarded as orthodox, and by his noble origination of the Christian Socialist movement.   The nearest parallel to him, in a moral point of view, is Coleridge, to whom, in merely intellectual power, apart from poetical genius, I think him decidedly superior.   At this time, however, he might be described as a disciple of Coleridge, and Sterling as a disciple of Coleridge and of him.   The modifications which were taking place in my old opinions gave me some points of contact with them; and both Maurice and Sterling were of considerable use to my development.   With Sterling I soon became very intimate, and was more attached to him than I have ever been to any other man.   He was indeed one of the most lovable of men.   His frank, cordial, affectionate, and expansive character; a love of truth alike conspicuous in the highest things and the humblest; a generous and ardent nature which threw itself with impetuosity into the opinions it adopted, but was as eager to do justice to the doctrines and the men it was opposed to, as to make war on what it thought their errors; and an equal devotion to the two cardinal points of Liberty and Duty, formed a combination of qualities as attractive to me, as to all others who knew him as well as I did. With his open mind and heart, he found no difficulty in joining hands with me across the gulf which as yet divided our opinions. He told me how he and others had looked upon me (from hearsay information), as a " made " or manufactured man, having had a certain impress of opinion stamped on me which I could only reproduce; and what a change took place in his feelings when he found, in the discussion on Wordsworth and Byron, that Wordsworth, and all which that name implies, " belonged " to me as much as to him and his friends. The failure of his health soon scattered all his plans of life, and compelled him to live at a distance from London, so that after the first year or two of our acquaintance, we only saw each other at distant intervals. But (as he said himself in one of his letters to Carlyle) when we did meet it was like brothers. Though he was never, in the full sense of the word, a profound thinker, his openness of mind, and the moral courage in which he greatly surpassed Maurice, made him outgrow the dominion which Maurice and Coleridge had once exercised over his intellect; though he retained to the last a great but discriminating admiration of both, and towards Maurice a warm affection. Except in that short and transitory phasis of his life, during which he made the mistake of becoming a clergyman, his mind was ever progressive: and the advance he always seemed to have made when I saw him after an interval, made me apply to him what Goethe said of Schiller, " Er hatte eine fürchterliche Fortschreitung." He and I started from intellectual points almost as wide apart as the poles, but the distance between us was always diminishing: if I made steps towards some of his opinions, he, during his short life, was constantly approximating more and more to several of mine: and if he had lived, and had health and vigour to prosecute his ever assiduous self-culture, there is no knowing how much further this spontaneous assimilation might have proceeded.

After 1829 I withdrew from attendance on the Debating Society. I had had enough of speech-making, and was glad to carry on my private studies and meditations without any immediate call for outward assertion of their results. I found the fabric of my old and taught opinions giving way in many fresh places, and I never allowed it to fall to pieces, but was incessantly occupied in weaving it anew. I never, in the course of my transition, was content to remain, for ever so short a time, confused and unsettled. When I had taken in any new idea, I could not rest till I had adjusted its relation to my old opinions, and ascertained exactly how far its effect ought to extend in modifying or superseding them.

The conflicts which I had so often had to sustain in defending the theory of government laid down in Bentham's and my father's writings, and the acquaintance I had obtained with other schools of political thinking, made me aware of many things which that doctrine, professing to be a theory of government in general, ought to have made room for, and did not. But these things, as yet, remained with me rather as corrections to be made in applying the theory to practice, than as defects in the theory. I felt that politics could not be a science of specific experience; and that the accusations against the Benthamic theory of *being* a theory, of proceeding *à priori* by way of general reasoning, instead of Baconian experiment, showed complete ignorance of Bacon's principles, and of the necessary conditions of experimental investigation. At this juncture appeared in the Edinburgh Review, Macaulay's famous attack on my father's Essay on Government. This gave me much to think about. I saw that Macaulay's conception

of the logic of politics was erroneous; that he stood up for
the empirical mode of treating political phenomena, against
the philosophical; that even in physical science his notion
of philosophizing might have recognized Kepler, but would
have excluded Newton and Laplace.   But I could not help
feeling, that though the tone was unbecoming (an error
for which the writer, at a later period, made the most ample
and honourable amends), there was truth in several of his
strictures on my father's treatment of the subject; that my
father's premises were really too narrow, and included but
a small number of the general truths, on which, in politics,
the important consequences depend.   Identity of interest between the governing body and the community at large, is
not, in any practical sense which can be attached to it, the
only thing on which good government depends; neither can
this identity of interest be secured by the mere conditions
of election.   I was not at all satisfied with the mode in
which my father met the criticisms of Macaulay.   He did
not, as I thought he ought to have done, justify himself
by saying, " I was not writing a scientific treatise on politics,
I was writing an argument for parliamentary reform."
He treated Macaulay's argument as simply irrational; an
attack upon the reasoning faculty; an example of the saying of Hobbes, that when reason is against a man, a man
will be against reason.   This made me think that there
was really something more fundamentally erroneous in my
father's conception of philosophical method, as applicable
to politics, than I had hitherto supposed there was.   But I
did not at first see clearly what the error might be.   At
last it flashed upon me all at once in the course of other
studies.   In the early part of 1830 I had begun to put on
paper the ideas on Logic (chiefly on the distinctions among
Terms, and the import of Propositions) which had been
suggested and in part worked out in the morning conversations already spoken of.   Having secured these thoughts
from being lost, I pushed on into the other parts of the

subject, to try whether I could do anything further towards
clearing up the theory of Logic generally. I grappled at
once with the problem of Induction, postponing that of
Reasoning, on the ground that it is necessary to obtain
premises before we can reason from them. Now, Induction is mainly a process for finding the causes of effects:
and in attempting to fathom the mode of tracing causes and
effects in physical science, I soon saw that in the more
perfect of the sciences, we ascend, by generalization from
particulars, to the tendencies of causes considered singly,
and then reason downward from those separate tendencies,
to the effect of the same causes when combined. I then
asked myself, what is the ultimate analysis of this deductive
process; the common theory of the syllogism evidently
throwing no light upon it. My practice (learnt from
Hobbes and my father) being to study abstract principles
by means of the best concrete instances I could find, the
Composition of Forces, in dynamics, occurred to me as the
most complete example of the logical process I was investi-
gating. On examining, accordingly, what the mind does
when it applies the principle of the Composition of Forces,
I found that it performs a simple act of addition. It adds
the separate effect of the one force to the separate effect of
the other, and puts down the sum of these separate effects
as the joint effect. But is this a legitimate process? In
dynamics, and in all the mathematical branches of physics,
it is; but in some other cases, as in chemistry, it is not; and
I then recollected that something not unlike this was pointed
out as one of the distinctions between chemical and
mechanical phenomena, in the introduction to that favourite
of my boyhood, Thomson's System of Chemistry. This
distinction at once made my mind clear as to what was per-
plexing me in respect to the philosophy of politics. I now
saw, that a science is either deductive or experimental,
according as, in the province it deals with, the effects of
causes when conjoined, are or are not the sums of the effects

which the same causes produce when separate. It followed that politics must be a deductive science. It thus appeared, that both Macaulay and my father were wrong; the one in assimilating the method of philosophizing in politics to the purely experimental method of chemistry; while the other, though right in adopting a deductive method, had made a wrong selection of one, having taken as the type of deduction, not the appropriate process, that of the deductive branches of natural philosophy, but the inappropriate one of pure geometry, which, not being a science of causation at all, does not require or admit of any summing-up of effects. A foundation was thus laid in my thoughts for the principal chapters of what I afterwards published on the Logic of the Moral Sciences; and my new position in respect to my old political creed, now became perfectly definite.

If I am asked, what system of political philosophy I substituted for that which, as a philosophy, I had abandoned, I answer, no system: only a conviction that the true system was something much more complex and many-sided than I had previously had any idea of, and that its office was to supply, not a set of model institutions, but principles from which the institutions suitable to any given circumstances might be deduced. The influences of European, that is to say, Continental, thought, and especially those of the reaction of the nineteenth century against the eighteenth, were now streaming in upon me. They came from various quarters: from the writings of Coleridge, which I had begun to read with interest even before the change in my opinions; from the Coleridgians with whom I was in personal intercourse; from what I had read of Goethe; from Carlyle's early articles in the Edinburgh and Foreign Reviews, though for a long time I saw nothing in these (as my father saw nothing in them to the last) but insane rhapsody. From these sources, and from the acquaintance I kept up with the French literature of the time, I derived, among other ideas which the general turning upside down of the opinions of European thinkers had brought uppermost, these in particular: That the human mind has a certain order of possible progress, in which some things must precede others, an order which governments and public instructors can modify to some, but not to an unlimited extent: That all questions of political institutions are relative, not absolute, and that different stages of human progress not only *will* have, but *ought* to have, different institutions: That government is always either in the hands, or passing into the hands, of whatever is the strongest power in society, and that what this power is, does not depend on institutions, but institutions on it: That any general theory or philosophy of politics supposes a previous theory of human progress, and that this is the same thing with a philosophy of history. These opinions, true in the main, were held in an exaggerated and violent manner by the thinkers with whom I was now most accustomed to compare notes, and who, as usual with a reaction, ignored that half of the truth which the thinkers of the eighteenth century saw. But though, at one period of my progress, I for some time undervalued that great century, I never joined in the reaction against it, but kept as firm hold of one side of the truth as I took of the other. The fight between the nineteenth century and the eighteenth always reminded me of the battle about the shield, one side of which was white and the other black. I marvelled at the blind rage with which the combatants rushed against one another. I applied to them, and to Coleridge himself, many of Coleridge's sayings about half truths; and Goethe's device, " many-sidedness," was one which I would most willingly, at this period, have taken for mine.

The writers by whom, more than by any others, a new mode of political thinking was brought home to me, were those of the St. Simonian school in France. In 1829 and 1830 I became acquainted with some of their writings.

They were then only in the earlier stages of their speculations. They had not yet dressed out their philosophy as a religion, nor had they organized their scheme of Socialism. They were just beginning to question the principle of hereditary property. I was by no means prepared to go with them even this length; but I was greatly struck with the connected view which they for the first time presented to me, of the natural order of human progress; and especially with their division of all history into organic periods and critical periods. During the organic periods (they said) mankind accept with firm conviction some positive creed, claiming jurisdiction over all their actions, and containing more or less of truth and adaptation to the needs of humanity. Under its influence they make all the progress compatible with the creed, and finally outgrow it; when a period follows of criticism and negation, in which mankind lose their old convictions without acquiring any new ones, of a general or authoritative character, except the conviction that the old are false. The period of Greek and Roman polytheism, so long as really believed in by instructed Greeks and Romans, was an organic period, succeeded by the critical or sceptical period of the Greek philosophers. Another organic period came in with Christianity. The corresponding critical period began with the Reformation, has lasted ever since, still lasts, and cannot altogether cease until a new organic period has been inaugurated by the triumph of a yet more advanced creed. These ideas, I knew, were not peculiar to the St. Simonians; on the contrary, they were the general property of Europe, or at least of Germany and France, but they had never, to my knowledge, been so completely systematized as by these writers, nor the distinguishing characteristics of a critical period so powerfully set forth; for I was not then acquainted with Fichte's Lectures on " the Characteristics of the Present Age." In Carlyle, indeed, I found bitter denunciations of an " age of unbelief," and of the present

age as such, which I, like most people at that time, supposed to be passionate protests in favour of the old modes
of belief. But all that was true in these denunciations, I
thought that I found more calmly and philosophically
stated by the St. Simonians. Among their publications,
too, there was one which seemed to me far superior to the
rest; in which the general idea was matured into something
much more definite and instructive. This was an early
work of Auguste Comte, who then called himself, and even
announced himself in the title-page as, a pupil of Saint-
Simon. In this tract M. Comte first put forth the doctrine,
which he afterwards so copiously illustrated, of the natural
succession of three stages in every department of human
knowledge: first, the theological, next the metaphysical, and
lastly, the positive stage; and contended, that social science
must be subject to the same law; that the feudal and
Catholic system was the concluding phasis of the theological state of the social science, Protestantism the commencement, and the doctrines of the French Revolution the
consummation of the metaphysical; and that its positive
state was yet to come. This doctrine harmonized well with
my existing notions, to which it seemed to give a scientific
shape. I already regarded the methods of physical science
as the proper models for political. But the chief benefit
which I derived at this time from the trains of thought
suggested by the St. Simonians and by Comte, was, that I
obtained a clearer conception than ever before of the
peculiarities of an era of transition in opinion, and ceased
to mistake the moral and intellectual characteristics of such
an era, for the normal attributes of humanity. I looked
forward, through the present age of loud disputes but
generally weak convictions, to a future which shall unite
the best qualities of the critical with the best qualities of
the organic periods; unchecked liberty of thought, unbounded freedom of individual action in all modes not
hurtful to others; but also, convictions as to what is right

and wrong, useful and pernicious, deeply engraven on the feelings by early education and general unanimity of sentiment, and so firmly grounded in reason and in the true exigencies of life, that they shall not, like all former and present creeds, religious, ethical, and political, require to be periodically thrown off and replaced by others.

M. Comte soon left the St. Simonians, and I lost sight of him and his writings for a number of years. But the St. Simonians I continued to cultivate. I was kept *au courant* of their progress by one of their most enthusiastic disciples, M. Gustave d'Eichthal, who about that time passed a considerable interval in England. I was introduced to their chiefs, Bazard and Enfantin, in 1830; and as long as their public teachings and proselytism continued, I read nearly everything they wrote. Their criticisms on the common doctrines of Liberalism seemed to me full of important truth; and it was partly by their writings that my eyes were opened to the very limited and temporary value of the old political economy, which assumes private property and inheritance as indefeasible facts, and freedom of production and exchange as the *dernier mot* of social improvement. The scheme gradually unfolded by the St. Simonians, under which the labour and capital of society would be managed for the general account of the community, every individual being required to take a share of labour, either as thinker, teacher, artist, or producer, all being classed according to their capacity, and remunerated according to their works, appeared to me a far superior description of Socialism to Owen's. Their aim seemed to me desirable and rational, however their means might be inefficacious; and though I neither believed in the practicability, nor in the beneficial operation of their social machinery, I felt that the proclamation of such an ideal of human society could not but tend to give a beneficial direction to the efforts of others to bring society, as at present constituted, nearer to some ideal standard. I honoured them most of all for what they have been most cried down for — the boldness and freedom from prejudice with which they treated the subject of family, the most important of any, and needing more fundamental alterations than remain to be made in any other great social institution, but on which scarcely any reformer has the courage to touch. In proclaiming the perfect equality of men and women, and an entirely new order of things in regard to their relations with one another, the St. Simonians, in common with Owen and Fourier, have entitled themselves to the grateful remembrance of future generations.

In giving an account of this period of my life, I have only specified such of my new impressions as appeared to me, both at the time and since, to be a kind of turning points, marking a definite progress in my mode of thought. But these few selected points give a very insufficient idea of the quantity of thinking which I carried on respecting a host of subjects during these years of transition. Much of this, it is true, consisted in rediscovering things known to all the world, which I had previously disbelieved, or disregarded. But the rediscovery was to me a discovery, giving me plenary possession of the truths, not as traditional platitudes, but fresh from their source: and it seldom failed to place them in some new light, by which they were reconciled with, and seemed to confirm while they modified, the truths less generally known which lay in my early opinions, and in no essential part of which I at any time wavered. All my new thinking only laid the foundation of these more deeply and strongly, while it often removed misapprehension and confusion of ideas which had perverted their effect. For example, during the later returns of my dejection, the doctrine of what is called Philosophical Necessity weighed on my existence like an incubus. I felt as if I was scientifically proved to be the helpless slave of antecedent circumstances; as if my character and that of all others had been formed for us by agencies beyond our control, and was wholly out of our own power. I often said to myself, what a relief it would be if I could disbelieve the doctrine of the formation of character by circumstances; and remembering the wish of Fox respecting the doctrine of resistance to governments, that it might never be forgotten by kings, nor remembered by subjects, I said that it would be a blessing if the doctrine of necessity could be believed by all *quoad* the characters of others, and disbelieved in regard to their own. I pondered painfully on the subject, till gradually I saw light through it. I perceived, that the word Necessity, as a name for the doctrine of Cause and Effect applied to human action, carried with it a misleading association; and that this association was the operative force in the depressing and paralysing influence which I had experienced: I saw that though our character is formed by circumstances, our own desires can do much to shape those circumstances; and that what is really inspiriting and ennobling in the doctrine of freewill, is the conviction that we have real power over the formation of our own character; that our will, by influencing some of our circumstances, can modify our future habits or capabilities of willing. All this was entirely consistent with the doctrine of circumstances, or rather, was that doctrine itself, properly understood. From that time I drew in my own mind, a clear distinction between the doctrine of circumstances, and Fatalism; discarding altogether the misleading word Necessity. The theory, which I now for the first time rightly apprehended, ceased altogether to be discouraging, and besides the relief to my spirits, I no longer suffered under the burthen, so heavy to one who aims at being a reformer in opinions, of thinking one doctrine true, and the contrary doctrine morally beneficial. The train of thought which had extricated me from this dilemma, seemed to me, in after years, fitted to render a similar service to others; and it now forms the chapter on Liberty and Necessity in the concluding Book of my " System of Logic."

Again, in politics, though I no longer accepted the doctrine of the Essay on Government as a scientific theory; though I ceased to consider representative democracy as an absolute principle, and regarded it as a question of time, place, and circumstance; though I now looked upon the choice of political institutions as a moral and educational question more than one of material interests, thinking that it ought to be decided mainly by the consideration, what great improvement in life and culture stands next in order for the people concerned, as the condition of their further progress, and what institutions are most likely to promote that; nevertheless, this change in the premises of my political philosophy did not alter my practical political creed as to the requirements of my own time and country. I was as much as ever a radical and democrat for Europe, and especially for England. I thought the predominance of the aristocratic classes, the noble and the rich, in the English Constitution, an evil worth any struggle to get rid of; not on account of taxes, or any such comparatively small inconvenience, but as the great demoralizing agency in the country. Demoralizing, first, because it made the conduct of the government an example of gross public immorality, through the predominance of private over public interests in the State, and the abuse of the powers of legislation for the advantage of classes. Secondly, and in a still greater degree, because the respect of the multitude always attaching itself principally to that which, in the existing state of society, is the chief passport to power; and under English institutions, riches, hereditary or acquired, being the almost exclusive source of political importance; riches, and the signs of riches, were almost the only things really respected, and the life of the people was mainly devoted to the pursuit of them. I thought, that while the higher and richer classes held the power of government, the instruction and improvement of the mass of the people were contrary to the self-interest of those classes, because tending to render the people more powerful for throwing off the yoke: but if the democracy obtained a large, and perhaps the principal, share in the governing power, it would become the interest of the opulent classes to promote their education, in order to ward off really mischievous errors, and especially those which would lead to unjust violations of property. On these grounds I was not only as ardent as ever for democratic institutions, but earnestly hoped that Owenite, St. Simonian, and all other anti-property doctrines might spread widely among the poorer classes; not that I thought those doctrines true, or desired that they should be acted on, but in order that the higher classes might be made to see that they had more to fear from the poor when uneducated, than when educated.

In this frame of mind the French Revolution of July found me. It aroused my utmost enthusiasm, and gave me, as it were, a new existence. I went at once to Paris, was introduced to Lafayette, and laid the groundwork of the intercourse I afterwards kept up with several of the active chiefs of the extreme popular party. After my return I entered warmly, as a writer, into the political discussions of the time; which soon became still more exciting, by the coming in of Lord Grey's ministry, and the proposing of the Reform Bill. For the next few years I wrote copiously in newspapers. It was about this time that Fonblanque, who had for some time written the political articles in the Examiner, became the proprietor and editor of the paper. It is not forgotten with what verve and talent, as well as fine wit, he carried it on, during the whole period of Lord Grey's ministry, and what importance it assumed as the principal representative, in the newspaper press, of radical opinions. The distinguishing character of the paper was given to it entirely by his own articles, which formed

at least three-fourths of all the original writing contained
in it: but of the remaining fourth I contributed during those
years a much larger share than any one else. I wrote
nearly all the articles on French subjects, including a
weekly summary of French politics, often extending to considerable length; together with many leading articles on
general politics, commercial and financial legislation, and
any miscellaneous subjects in which I felt interested, and
which were suitable to the paper, including occasional reviews of books. Mere newspaper articles on the occurrences or questions of the moment, gave no opportunity for
the development of any general mode of thought; but I
attempted, in the beginning of 1831, to emb..y in a series
of articles, headed " The Spirit of the Age," some of my
new opinions, and especially to point out in the character
of the present age, the anomalies and evils characteristic
of the transition from a system of opinions which had worn
out, to another only in process of being formed. These
articles were, I fancy, lumbering in style, and not lively
or striking enough to be at any time, acceptable to newspaper readers; but had they been far more attractive, still,
at that particular moment, when great political changes
were impending, and engrossing all minds, these discussions
were ill-timed, and missed fire altogether. The only effect
which I know to have been produced by them, was that
Carlyle, then living in a secluded part of Scotland, read
them in his solitude, and saying to himself (as he afterwards told me) " here is a new Mystic," inquired on coming
to London that autumn respecting their authorship; an
inquiry which was the immediate cause of our becoming
personally acquainted.

I have already mentioned Carlyle's earlier writings as
one of the channels through which I received the influences
which enlarged my early narrow creed; but I do not think
that those writings, by themselves, would ever have had
any effect on my opinions. What truths they contained,

though of the very kind which I was already receiving from other quarters, were presented in a form and vesture less suited than any other to give them access to a mind trained as mine had been. They seemed a haze of poetry and German metaphysics, in which almost the only clear thing was a strong animosity to most of the opinions which were the basis of my mode of thought; religious scepticism, utilitarianism, the doctrine of circumstances, and the attaching any importance to democracy, logic, or political economy. Instead of my having been taught anything, in the first instance, by Carlyle, it was only in proportion as I came to see the same truths through media more suited to my mental constitution, that I recognized them in his writings. Then, indeed, the wonderful power with which he put them forth made a deep impression upon me, and I was during a long period one of his most fervent admirers; but the good his writings did me, was not as philosophy to instruct, but as poetry to animate. Even at the time when our acquaintance commenced, I was not sufficiently advanced in my new modes of thought, to appreciate him fully; a proof of which is, that on his showing me the manuscript of Sartor Resartus, his best and greatest work, which he had just then finished, I made little of it; though when it came out about two years afterwards in Fraser's Magazine I read it with enthusiastic admiration and the keenest delight. I did not seek and cultivate Carlyle less on account of the fundamental differences in our philosophy. He soon found out that I was not "another mystic," and when for the sake of my own integrity I wrote to him a distinct profession of all those of my opinions which I knew he most disliked, he replied that the chief difference between us was that I "was as yet consciously nothing of a mystic." I do not know at what period he gave up the expectation that I was destined to become one; but though both his and my opinions underwent in subsequent years considerable changes, we never approached much nearer to each other's modes of

thought than we were in the first years of our acquaintance.
I did not, however, deem myself a competent judge of
Carlyle. I felt that he was a poet, and that I was not; that
he was a man of intuition, which I was not; and that as
such, he not only saw many things long before me, which
I could only when they were pointed out to me, hobble
after and prove, but that it was highly probable he could
see many things which were not visible to me even after
they were pointed out. I knew that I could not see round
him, and could never be certain that I saw over him; and
I never presumed to judge him with any definiteness,
until he was interpreted to me by one greatly the superior
of us both — who was more a poet than he, and more a
thinker than I — whose own mind and nature included
his, and infinitely more.

Among the persons of intellect whom I had known of
old, the one with whom I had now most points of agreement was the elder Austin. I have mentioned that he
always set himself in opposition to our early sectarianism;
and latterly he had, like myself, come under new influences.
Having been appointed Professor of Jurisprudence in the
London University (now University College), he had
lived for some time at Bonn to study for his Lectures; and
the influences of German literature and of the German
character and state of society had made a very perceptible
change in his views of life. His personal disposition was
much softened; he was less militant and polemic; his tastes
had begun to turn themselves towards the poetic and contemplative. He attached much less importance than formerly to outward changes; unless accompanied by a better
cultivation of the inward nature. He had a strong distaste
for the general meanness of English life, the absence of
enlarged thoughts and unselfish desires, the low objects on
which the faculties of all classes of the English are intent.
Even the kind of public interests which Englishmen care
for, he held in very little esteem. He thought that there

was more practical good government, and (which is true enough) infinitely more care for the education and mental improvement of all ranks of the people, under the Prussian monarchy, than under the English representative government: and he held, with the French Economistes, that the real security for good government is "un peuple éclairé," which is not always the fruit of popular institutions, and which if it could be had without them, would do their work better than they. Though he approved of the Reform Bill, he predicted, what in fact occurred, that it would not produce the great immediate improvements in government, which many expected from it. The men, he said, who could do these great things, did not exist in the country. There were many points of sympathy between him and me, both in the new opinions he had adopted and in the old ones which he retained. Like me, he never ceased to be an utilitarian, and with all his love of the Germans, and enjoyment of their literature, never became in the smallest degree reconciled to the innate-principle metaphysics. He cultivated more and more a kind of German religion, a religion of poetry and feeling with little, if anything, of positive dogma; while, in politics (and here it was that I most differed with him) he acquired an indifference, bordering on contempt, for the progress of popular institutions: though he rejoiced in that of Socialism, as the most effectual means of compelling the powerful classes to educate the people, and to impress on them the only real means of permanently improving their material condition, a limitation of their numbers. Neither was he, at this time, fundamentally opposed to Socialism in itself as an ultimate result of improvement. He professed great disrespect for what he called "the universal principles of human nature of the political economists," and insisted on the evidence which history and daily experience afford of the "extraordinary pliability of human nature" (a phrase which I have somewhere borrowed from him); nor did he think it possible to set any positive bounds to the moral capabilities which might unfold themselves in mankind, under an enlightened direction of social and educational influences. Whether he retained all these opinions to the end of life I know not. Certainly the modes of thinking of his later years, and especially of his last publication, were much more Tory in their general character than those which he held at this time.

My father's tone of thought and feeling, I now felt myself at a great distance from: greater, indeed, than a full and calm explanation and reconsideration on both sides, might have shown to exist in reality. But my father was not one with whom calm and full explanations on fundamental points of doctrine could be expected, at least with one whom he might consider as, in some sort, a deserter from his standard. Fortunately we were almost always in strong agreement on the political questions of the day which engrossed a large part of his interest and of his conversation. On those matters of opinion on which we differed, we talked little. He knew that the habit of thinking for myself, which his mode of education had fostered, sometimes led me to opinions different from his, and he perceived from time to time that I did not always tell him *how* different. I expected no good, but only pain to both of us, from discussing our differences: and I never expressed them but when he gave utterance to some opinion of feeling repugnant to mine, in a manner which would have made it disingenuousness on my part to remain silent.

It remains to speak of what I wrote during these years, which, independently of my contributions to newspapers, was considerable. In 1830 and 1831 I wrote the five Essays since published under the title of " Essays on some Unsettled Questions of Political Economy," almost as they now stand, except that in 1833 I partially rewrote the fifth Essay. They were written with no immediate purpose of publication; and when, some years later, I offered them to a publisher, he declined them. They were only printed in

1844, after the success of the "System of Logic." I also resumed my speculations on this last subject, and puzzled myself, like others before me, with the great paradox of the discovery of new truths by general reasoning. As to the fact, there could be no doubt. As little could it be doubted, that all reasoning is resolvable into syllogisms, and that in every syllogism the conclusion is actually contained and implied in the premises. How, being so contained and implied, it could be new truth, and how the theorems of geometry, so different in appearance from the definitions and axioms, could be all contained in these, was a difficulty which no one, I thought, had sufficiently felt, and which, at all events, no one had succeeded in clearing up. The explanations offered by Whately and others, though they might give a temporary satisfaction, always, in my mind, left a mist still hanging over the subject. At last, when reading a second or third time the chapters on Reasoning in the second volume of Dugald Stewart, interrogating myself on every point, and following out, as far as I knew how, every topic of thought which the book suggested, I came upon an idea of his respecting the use of axioms in ratiocination, which I did not remember to have before noticed, but which now, in meditating on it, seemed to me not only true of axioms, but of all general propositions whatever, and to be the key of the whole perplexity. From this germ grew the theory of the Syllogism propounded in the Second Book of the Logic; which I immediately fixed by writing it out. And now, with greatly increased hope of being able to produce a work on Logic, of some originality and value, I proceeded to write the First Book, from the rough and imperfect draft I had already made. What I now wrote became the basis of that part of the subsequent Treatise; except that it did not contain the Theory of Kinds, which was a later addition, suggested by otherwise inextricable difficulties which met me in my first attempt to work out the subject of some of the concluding chapters of the Third Book. At the point which I had now reached I made a halt, which lasted five years. I had come to the end of my tether; I could make nothing satisfactory of Induction, at this time. I continued to read any book which seemed to promise light on the subject, and appropriated, as well as I could, the results; but for a long time I found nothing which seemed to open to me any very important vein of meditation.

In 1832 I wrote several papers for the first series of Tait's Magazine, and one for a quarterly periodical called the Jurist, which had been founded, and for a short time carried on, by a set of friends, all lawyers and law reformers, with several of whom I was acquainted. The paper in question is the one on the rights and duties of the State respecting Corporation and Church Property, now standing first among the collected " Dissertations and Discussions; " where one of my articles in Tait, " The Currency Juggle," also appears. In the whole mass of what I wrote previous to these, there is nothing of sufficient permanent value to justify reprinting. The paper in the Jurist, which I still think a very complete discussion of the rights of the State over Foundations, showed both sides of my opinions, asserting as firmly as I should have done at any time, the doctrine that all endowments are national property, which the government may and ought to control; but not, as I should once have done, condemning endowments in themselves, and proposing that they should be taken to pay off the national debt. On the contrary, I urged strenuously the importance of having a provision for education, not dependent on the mere demand of the market, that is, on the knowledge and discernment of average parents, but calculated to establish and keep up a higher standard of instruction than is likely to be spontaneously demanded by the buyers of the article. All these opinions have been confirmed and strengthened by the whole course of my subsequent reflections.

CHAPTER VI

COMMENCEMENT OF THE MOST VALUABLE
FRIENDSHIP OF MY LIFE. MY FATHER'S
DEATH. WRITINGS AND OTHER PROCEED-
INGS UP TO 1840.

IT was at the period of my mental progress which I have
now reached that I formed the friendship which has
been the honour and chief blessing of my existence, as well
as the source of a great part of all that I have attempted
to do, or hope to effect hereafter, for human improvement.
My first introduction to the lady who, after a friendship of
twenty years, consented to become my wife, was in 1830,
when I was in my twenty-fifth and she in her twenty-third
year. With her husband's family it was the renewal of an
old acquaintanceship. His grandfather lived in the next
house to my father's in Newington Green, and I had sometimes when a boy been invited to play in the old gentle-
man's garden. He was a fine specimen of the old Scotch
puritan; stern, severe, and powerful, but very kind to
children, on whom such men make a lasting impression.
Although it was years after my introduction to Mrs. Taylor
before my acquaintance with her became at all intimate or
confidential, I very soon felt her to be the most admirable
person I had ever known. It is not to be supposed that she
was, or that any one, at the age at which I first saw her,
could be, all that she afterwards became. Least of all
could this be true of her, with whom self-improvement,
progress in the highest and in all senses, was a law of her
nature; a necessity equally from the ardour with which she
sought it, and from the spontaneous tendency of faculties
which could not receive an impression or an experience

without making it the source or the occasion of an accession of wisdom. Up to the time when I first saw her, her rich and powerful nature had chiefly unfolded itself according to the received type of feminine genius. To her outer circle she was a beauty and a wit, with an air of natural distinction, felt by all who approached her: to the inner, a woman of deep and strong feeling, of penetrating and intuitive intelligence, and of an eminently meditative and poetic nature. Married at a very early age, to a most upright, brave, and honourable man, of liberal opinions and good education, but without the intellectual or [1] artistic tastes which would have made him a companion for her, though a steady and affectionate friend, for whom she had true esteem and the strongest affection through life, and whom she most deeply lamented when dead; shut out by the social disabilities of women from any adequate exercise of her highest faculties in action on the world without; her life was one of inward meditation, varied by familiar intercourse with a small circle of friends, of whom [2] one only (long since deceased) was a person of genius, or of capacities of feeling or intellect kindred with her own, but all had more or less of alliance with her in sentiments and opinions. Into this circle I had the good fortune to be admitted, and I soon perceived that she possessed in combination, the qualities which in all other persons whom I had known I had been only too happy to find singly. In her, complete emancipation from every kind of superstition (including that which attributes a pretended perfection to the order of nature and the universe), and an earnest protest against many things which are still part of the established constitution of society, resulted not from the hard intellect, but from strength of noble and elevated feeling, and co-existed with a highly reverential nature. In general spiritual characteristics, as well as in

[1] Pencil note by H. T. on MS. "not true."
[2] Pencil note on MS. "Miss Flower, H. T."

temperament and organisation, I have often compared her, as she was at this time, to Shelley: but in thought and intellect, Shelley, so far as his powers were developed in his short life, was but a child compared with what she ultimately became.   Alike in the highest regions of speculation and in the smaller practical concerns of daily life, her mind was the same perfect instrument, piercing to the very heart and marrow of the matter; always seizing the essential idea or principle.   The same exactness and rapidity of operation, pervading as it did her sensitive as well as her mental faculties, would, with her gifts of feeling and imagination, have fitted her to be a consummate artist, as her fiery and tender soul and her vigorous eloquence would certainly have made her a great orator, and her profound knowledge of human nature and discernment and sagacity in practical life, would, in the times when such a *carrière* was open to women, have made her eminent among the rulers of mankind.   Her intellectual gifts did but minister to a moral character at once the noblest and the best balanced which I have ever met with in life.   Her unselfishness was not that of a taught system of duties, but of a heart which thoroughly identified itself with the feelings of others, and often went to excess in consideration for them by imaginatively investing their feelings with the intensity of its own.   The passion of justice might have been thought to be her strongest feeling, but for her boundless generosity, and a lovingness ever ready to pour itself forth upon any or all human beings who were capable of giving the smallest feeling in return. The rest of her moral characteristics were such as naturally accompany these qualities of mind and heart: the most genuine modesty combined with the loftiest pride; a simplicity and sincerity which were absolute, towards all who were fit to receive them; the utmost scorn of whatever was mean and cowardly, and a burning indignation at everything brutal or tyrannical, faithless or dishonourable in conduct and character, while making the broadest distinction between *mala in se* and mere *mala prohibita* — between acts giving evidence of intrinsic badness in feeling and character, and those which are only violations of conventions either good or bad, violations which whether in themselves right or wrong, are capable of being committed by persons in every other respect lovable or admirable.

To be admitted into any degree of mental intercourse with a being of these qualities, could not but have a most beneficial influence on my development; though the effect was only gradual, and many years elapsed before her mental progress and mine went forward in the complete companionship they at last attained. The benefit I received was far greater than any which I could hope to give; though to her, who had at first reached her opinions by the moral intuition of a character of strong feeling, there was doubtless help as well as encouragement to be derived from one who had arrived at many of the same results by study and reasoning: and in the rapidity of her intellectual growth, her mental activity, which converted everything into knowledge, doubtless drew from me, as it did from other sources, many of its materials. What I owe, even intellectually, to her, is in its detail, almost infinite; of its general character a few words will give some, though a very imperfect, idea. With those who, like all the best and wisest of mankind, are dissatisfied with human life as it is, and whose feelings are wholly identified with its radical amendment, there are two main regions of thought. One is the region of ultimate aims; the constituent elements of the highest realizable ideal of human life. The other is that of the immediately useful and practically attainable. In both these departments, I have acquired more from her teaching, than from all other sources taken together. And, to say truth, it is in these two extremes principally, that real certainty lies. My own strength lay wholly in the uncertain and slippery intermediate region, that of theory, or moral and political science: respecting the conclusions of which, in any of the forms in which I have received or originated them, whether as political economy, analytic psychology, logic, philosophy of history, or anything else, it is not the least of my intellectual obligations to her that I have derived from her a wise scepticism, which, while it has not hindered me from following out the honest exercise of my thinking faculties to whatever conclusions might result from it, has put me on my guard against holding or announcing these conclusions with a degree of confidence which the nature of such speculations does not warrant, and has kept my mind not only open to admit, but prompt to welcome and eager to seek, even on the questions on which I have most meditated, any prospect of clearer perceptions and better evidence. I have often received praise, which in my own right I only partially deserve, for the greater practicality which is supposed to be found in my writings, compared with those of most thinkers who have been equally addicted to large generalizations. The writings in which this quality has been observed, were not the work of one mind, but of the fusion of two, one of them as pre-eminently practical in its judgments and perceptions of things present, as it was high and bold in its anticipations for a remote futurity.

At the present period, however, this influence was only one among many which were helping to shape the character of my future development: and even after it became, I may truly say, the presiding principle of my mental progress, it did not alter the path, but only made me move forward more boldly, and, at the same time, more cautiously, in the same course. The only actual revolution which has ever taken place in my modes of thinking, was already complete. My new tendencies had to be confirmed in some respects, moderated in others: but the only substantial changes of opinion that were yet to come, related to politics, and consisted, on one hand, in a greater approximation, so far as regards the ultimate prospects of humanity, to a qualified

Socialism, and on the other, a shifting of my political ideal from pure democracy, as commonly understood by its partizans, to the modified form of it, which is set forth in my " Considerations on Representative Government."

This last change, which took place very gradually, dates its commencement from my reading, or rather study, of M. de Tocqueville's " Democracy in America," which fell into my hands immediately after its first appearance. In that remarkable work, the excellences of Democracy were pointed out in a more conclusive, because a more specific manner than I had ever known them to be, even by the most enthusiastic democrats; while the specific dangers which beset Democracy, considered as the government of the numerical majority, were brought into equally strong light, and subjected to a masterly analysis, not as reasons for resisting what the author considered as an inevitable result of human progress, but as indications of the weak points of popular government, the defences by which it needs to be guarded, and the correctives which must be added to it in order that while full play is given to its beneficial tendencies, those which are of a different nature may be neutralized or mitigated. I was now well prepared for speculations of this character, and from this time onward my own thoughts moved more and more in the same channel, though the consequent modifications in my practical political creed were spread over many years, as would be shown by comparing my first review of " Democracy in America," written and published in 1835, with the one in 1840 (reprinted in the " Dissertations "), and this last, with the " Considerations on Representative Government."

A collateral subject on which also I derived great benefit from the study of Tocqueville, was the fundamental question of Centralization. The powerful philosophic analysis which he applied to American and to French experience, led him to attach the utmost importance to the performance of as much of the collective business of society, as can safely

be so performed, by the people themselves, without any
intervention of the executive government, either to super-
sede their agency, or to dictate the manner of its exercise.
He viewed this practical political activity of the individual
citizen, not only as one of the most effectual means of training the social feelings and practical intelligence of the
people, so important in themselves and so indispensable to
good government, but also as the specific counteractive to
some of the characteristic infirmities of Democracy, and a
necessary protection against its degenerating into the only
despotism of which, in the modern world, there is real
danger — the absolute rule of the head of the executive
over a congregation of isolated individuals, all equals but
all slaves.   There was, indeed, no immediate peril from
this source on the British side of the channel, where nine-
tenths of the internal business which elsewhere devolves
on the government, was transacted by agencies independent
of it; where Centralization was, and is, the subject not only
of rational disapprobation, but of unreasoning prejudice;
where jealousy of Government interference was a blind
feeling preventing or resisting even the most beneficial
exertion of legislative authority to correct the abuses of
what pretends to be local self-government, but is, too often,
selfish mismanagement of local interests, by a jobbing and
borné local oligarchy.   But the more certain the public
were to go wrong on the side opposed to Centralization, the
greater danger was there lest philosophic reformers should
fall into the contrary error, and overlook the mischiefs of
which they had been spared the painful experience.   I was
myself, at this very time, actively engaged in defending
important measures, such as the great Poor Law Reform
of 1834, against an irrational clamour grounded on the
Anti-Centralization prejudice: and had it not been for the
lessons of Tocqueville, I do not know that I might not,
like many reformers before me, have been hurried into the
excess opposite to that, which, being the one prevalent in my

own country, it was generally my business to combat. As it is, I have steered carefully between the two errors, and whether I have or have not drawn the line between them exactly in the right place, I have at least insisted with equal emphasis upon the evils on both sides, and have made the means of reconciling the advantages of both, a subject of serious study.

In the meanwhile had taken place the election of the first Reformed Parliament, which included several of the most notable of my Radical friends and acquaintances — Grote, Roebuck, Buller, Sir William Molesworth, John and Edward Romilly, and several more; besides Warburton, Strutt, and others, who were in parliament already. Those who thought themselves, and were called by their friends, the philosophic radicals, had now, it seemed, a fair opportunity, in a more advantageous position than they had ever before occupied, for showing what was in them; and I, as well as my father, founded great hopes on them. These hopes were destined to be disappointed. The men were honest, and faithful to their opinions, as far as votes were concerned; often in spite of much discouragement. When measures were proposed, flagrantly at variance with their principles, such as the Irish Coercion Bill, or the Canada coercion in 1837, they came forward manfully, and braved any amount of hostility and prejudice rather than desert the right. But on the whole they did very little to promote any opinions; they had little enterprise, little activity: they left the lead of the radical portion of the House to the old hands, to Hume and O'Connell. A partial exception must be made in favour of one or two of the younger men; and in the case of Roebuck, it is his title to permanent remembrance, that in the very first year during which he sat in Parliament, he originated (or re-originated after the unsuccessful attempt of Mr. Brougham) the parliamentary movement for National Education; and that he was the first to commence, and for years carried on almost alone, the contest for the self-government of the Colonies.   Nothing, on the whole equal to these two things, was done by any other individual, even of those from whom most was expected.   And now, on a calm retrospect, I can perceive that the men were less in fault than we supposed, and that we had expected too much from them.   They were in unfavourable circumstances.   Their lot was cast in the ten years of inevitable reaction, when, the Reform excitement being over, and the few legislative improvements which the public really called for having been rapidly effected, power gravitated back in its natural direction, to those who were for keeping things as they were; when the public mind desired rest, and was less disposed than at any other period since the peace, to let itself be moved by attempts to work up the reform feeling into fresh activity in favour of new things.   It would have required a great political leader, which no one is to be blamed for not being, to have effected really great things by parliamentary discussion when the nation was in this mood. My father and I had hoped that some competent leader might arise; some man of philosophic attainments and popular talents, who could have put heart into the many younger or less distinguished men that would have been ready to join him — could have made them available, to the extent of their talents, in bringing advanced ideas before the public — could have used the House of Commons as a rostra or a teacher's chair for instructing and impelling the public mind; and would either have forced the Whigs to receive their measures from him, or have taken the lead of the Reform party out of their hands. Such a leader there would have been, if my father had been in Parliament.   For want of such a man, the instructed Radicals sank into a mere *côté gauche* of the Whig party. With a keen, and as I now think, an exaggerated sense of the possibilities which were open to the Radicals if they made even ordinary exertion for their opinions, I laboured from this time till 1839, both by personal influence with some of them, and by writings, to put ideas into their heads, and purpose into their hearts. I did some good with Charles Buller, and some with Sir William Molesworth; both of whom did valuable service, but were unhappily cut off almost in the beginning of their usefulness. On the whole, however, my attempt was vain. To have had a chance of succeeding in it, required a different position from mine. It was a task only for one who, being himself in Parliament, could have mixed with the radical members in daily consultation, could himself have taken the initiative, and instead of urging others to lead, could have summoned them to follow.

What I could do by writing, I did. During the year 1833 I continued working in the Examiner with Fonblanque who at that time was zealous in keeping up the fight for radicalism against the Whig ministry. During the session of 1834 I wrote comments on passing events, of the nature of newspaper articles (under the title " Notes on the Newspapers "), in the Monthly Repository, a magazine conducted by Mr. Fox, well known as a preacher and political orator, and subsequently as member of parliament for Oldham; with whom I had lately became acquainted, and for whose sake chiefly I wrote in his Magazine. I contributed several other articles to this periodical, the most considerable of which (on the theory of poetry), is reprinted in the " Dissertations." Altogether, the writings (independently of those in newspapers) which I published from 1832 to 1834, amount to a large volume. This, however, includes abstracts of several of Plato's Dialogues, with introductory remarks, which, though not published until 1834, had been written several years earlier; and which I afterwards, on various occasions, found to have been read, and their authorship known, by more people than were aware of anything else which I had written, up to that time. To complete the tale of my writings at this period, I may add that in 1833, at the request of Bulwer, who was just then completing his " England and the English " (a work, at that time, greatly in advance of the public mind), I wrote for him a critical account of Bentham's philosophy, a small part of which he incorporated in his text, and printed the rest (with an honourable acknowledgment), as an appendix. In this, along with the favourable, a part also of the unfavourable side of my estimation of Bentham's doctrines, considered as a complete philosophy, was for the first time put into print.

But an opportunity soon offered, by which, as it seemed, I might have it in my power to give more effectual aid, and, at the same time, stimulus, to the " philosophic radical " party, than I had done hitherto. One of the projects occasionally talked of between my father and me, and some of the parliamentary and other Radicals who frequented his house, was the foundation of a periodical organ of philosophic radicalism, to take the place which the Westminster Review had been intended to fill: and the scheme had gone so far as to bring under discussion the pecuniary contributions which could be looked for, and the choice of an editor. Nothing, however, came of it for some time: but in the summer of 1834 Sir William Molesworth, himself a laborious student, and a precise and metaphysical thinker, capable of aiding the cause by his pen as well as by his purse, spontaneously proposed to establish a Review, provided I would consent to be the real, if I could not be the ostensible, editor. Such a proposal was not to be refused; and the review was founded, at first under the title of the London Review, and afterwards under that of the London and Westminster, Molesworth having bought the Westminster from its proprietor, General Thompson, and merged the two into one. In the years between 1834 and 1840 the conduct of this review occupied the greater part of my spare time. In the beginning, it did not, as a whole, by any means represent my opinions. I was under the necessity of conceding much to my inevitable associates.

The Review was established to be the representative of the
" philosophic radicals," with most of whom I was now at
issue on many essential points, and among whom I could
not even claim to be the most important individual.   My
father's co-operation as a, writer we all deemed indispensable, and he wrote largely in it until prevented by his
last illness.   The subjects of his articles, and the strength
and decision with which his opinions were expressed in
them, made the Review at first derive its tone and colouring
from him much more than from any of the other writers.
I could not exercise editorial control over his articles, and I
was sometimes obliged to sacrifice to him portions of my
own.   The old Westminster Review doctrines, but little
modified, thus formed the staple of the review; but I
hoped by the side of these, to introduce other ideas and
another tone, and to obtain for my own shade of opinion
a fair representation, along with those of other members
of the party.   With this end chiefly in view, I made it one
of the peculiarities of the work that every article should
bear an initial, or some other signature, and be held to
express the opinions solely of the individual writer; the
editor being only responsible for its being worth publishing and not in conflict with the objects for which the Review
was set on foot.   I had an opportunity of putting in practice my scheme of conciliation between the old and the new
" philosophic radicalism," by the choice of a subject for my
own first contribution.   Professor Sedgwick, a man of
eminence in a particular walk of natural science, but who
should not have trespassed into philosophy, had lately
published his Discourse on the Studies of Cambridge, which
had as its most prominent feature an intemperate assault on
analytic psychology and utilitarian ethics, in the form of
an attack on Locke and Paley.   This had excited great
indignation in my father and others, which I thought it
fully deserved.   And here, I imagined, was an opportunity
of at the same time repelling an unjust attack, and insert-

ing into my defence of Hartleianism and Utilitarianism a number of the opinions which constituted my view of those subjects, as distinguished from that of my old associates. In this I partially succeeded, though my relation to my father would have made it painful to me in any case, and impossible in a review for which he wrote, to speak out my whole mind on the subject at this time.

I am, however, inclined to think that my father was not so much opposed as he seemed, to the modes of thought in which I believed myself to differ from him; that he did injustice to his own opinions by the unconscious exaggerations of an intellect emphatically polemical; and that when thinking without an adversary in view, he was willing to make room for a great portion of the truths he seemed to deny. I have frequently observed that he made large allowance in practice for considerations which seemed to have no place in his theory. His " Fragment on Mackintosh," which he wrote and published about this time, although I greatly admired some parts of it, I read as a whole with more pain than pleasure; yet on reading it again, long after, I found little in the opinions it contains, but what I think in the main just; and I can even sympathize in his disgust at the *verbiage* of Mackintosh, though his asperity towards it went not only beyond what was judicious, but beyond what was even fair. One thing, which I thought, at the time, of good augury, was the very favourable reception he gave to Tocqueville's " Democracy in America." It is true, he said and thought much more about what Tocqueville said in favour of Democracy, than about what he said of its disadvantages. Still, his high appreciation of a book which was at any rate an example of a mode of treating the question of government almost the reverse of his — wholly inductive and analytical, instead of purely ratiocinative — gave me great encouragement. He also approved of an article which I published in the first number following the junction of the two reviews, the essay reprinted in the Dissertations, under the title " Civilization; " into which I threw many of my new opinions, and criticised rather emphatically the mental and moral tendencies of the time, on grounds and in a manner which I certainly had not learnt from him.

All speculation, however, on the possible future developments of my father's opinions, and on the probabilities of permanent co-operation between him and me in the promulgation of our thoughts, was doomed to be cut short. During the whole of 1835 his health had been declining: his symptoms became unequivocally those of pulmonary consumption, and after lingering to the last stage of debility, he died on the 23rd of June, 1836. Until the last few days of his life there was no apparent abatement of intellectual vigour; his interest in all things and persons that had interested him through life was undiminished, nor did the approach of death cause the smallest wavering (as in so strong and firm a mind it was impossible that it should) in his convictions on the subject of religion. His principal satisfaction, after he knew that his end was near, seemed to be the thought of what he had done to make the world better than he found it; and his chief regret in not living longer, that he had not had time to do more.

His place is an eminent one in the literary, and even in the political history of his country; and it is far from honourable to the generation which has benefited by his worth, that he is so seldom mentioned, and, compared with men far his inferiors, so little remembered. This is probably to be ascribed mainly to two causes. In the first place, the thought of him merges too much in the deservedly superior fame of Bentham. Yet he was anything but Bentham's mere follower or disciple. Precisely because he was himself one of the most original thinkers of his time, he was one of the earliest to appreciate and adopt the most important mass of original thought which had been produced by the generation preceding him. His mind and Bentham's were essentially of different construction. He had not all Bentham's high qualities, but neither had Bentham all his. It would, indeed, be ridiculous to claim for him the praise of having accomplished for mankind such splendid services as Bentham's. He did not revolutionize, or rather create, one of the great departments of human thought. But, leaving out of the reckoning all that portion of his labours in which he benefited by what Bentham had done, and counting only what he achieved in a province in which Bentham had done nothing, that of analytic psychology, he will be known to posterity as one of the greatest names in that most important branch of speculation, on which all the moral and political sciences ultimately rest, and will mark one of the essential stages in its progress. The other reason which has made his fame less than he deserved, is that notwithstanding the great number of his opinions which, partly through his own efforts, have now been generally adopted, there was, on the whole, a marked opposition between his spirit and that of the present time. As Brutus was called the last of the Romans, so was he the last of the eighteenth century: he continued its tone of thought and sentiment into the nineteenth (though not unmodified nor unimproved), partaking neither in the good nor in the bad influences of the reaction against the eighteenth century, which was the great characteristic of the first half of the nineteenth. The eighteenth century was a great age, an age of strong and brave men, and he was a fit companion for its strongest and bravest. By his writings and his personal influence he was a great centre of light to his generation. During his later years he was quite as much the head and leader of the intellectual radicals in England, as Voltaire was of the *philosophes* of France. It is only one of his minor merits, that he was the originator of all sound statesmanship in regard to the subject of his largest work, India. He wrote on no subject which he did not enrich with valuable thought, and excepting the "Elements of Political Economy," a very useful book when first written, but which has now for some time finished its work, it will be long before any of his books will be wholly superseded, or will cease to be instructive reading to students of their subjects. In the power of influencing by mere force of mind and character, the convictions and purposes of others, and in the strenuous exertion of that power to promote freedom and progress, he left, as far as my knowledge extends, no equal among men and but one among women.

Though acutely sensible of my own inferiority in the qualities by which he acquired his personal ascendancy, I had now to try what it might be possible for me to accomplish without him: and the Review was the instrument on which I built my chief hopes of establishing a useful influence over the liberal and democratic section of the public mind. Deprived of my father's aid, I was also exempted from the restraints and reticences by which that aid had been purchased. I did not feel that there was any other radical writer or politician to whom I was bound to defer, further than consisted with my own opinions: and having the complete confidence of Molesworth, I resolved henceforth to give full scope to my own opinions and modes of thought, and to open the Review widely to all writers who were in sympathy with Progress as I understood it, even though I should lose by it the support of my former associates. Carlyle, consequently, became from this time a frequent writer in the Review; Sterling, soon after, an occasional one; and though each individual article continued to be the expression of the private sentiments of its writer, the general tone conformed in some tolerable degree to my opinions. For the conduct of the Review, under, and in conjunction with me, I associated with myself a young Scotchman of the name of Robertson, who had some ability and information, much industry, and an active scheming head, full of devices for making the Review more saleable, and on whose capacities in that direction I founded a good deal of hope: insomuch, that when Molesworth, in the beginning of 1837, became tired of carrying on the Review at a loss, and desirous of getting rid of it (he had done *his* part honourably, and at no small pecuniary cost,) I, very imprudently for my own pecuniary interest, and very much from reliance on Robertson's devices, determined to continue it at my own risk, until his plans should have had a fair trial. The devices were good, and I never had any reason to change my opinion of them. But I do not believe that any devices would have made a radical and democratic review defray its expenses, including a paid editor or sub-editor, and a liberal payment to writers. I myself and several frequent contributors gave our labour gratuitously, as we had done for Molesworth; but the paid contributors continued to be remunerated on the usual scale of the Edinburgh and Quarterly Reviews; and this could not be done from the proceeds of the sale.

In the same year, 1837, and in the midst of these occupations, I resumed the Logic. I had not touched my pen on the subject for five years, having been stopped and brought to a halt on the threshold of Induction. I had gradually discovered that what was mainly wanting, to overcome the difficulties of that branch of the subject, was a comprehensive, and, at the same time, accurate view of the whole circle of physical science, which I feared it would take me a long course of study to acquire; since I knew not of any book, or other guide, that would spread out before me the generalities and processes of the sciences, and I apprehended that I should have no choice but to extract them for myself, as I best could, from the details. Happily for me, Dr. Whewell, early in this year, published his History of the Inductive Sciences. I read it with eagerness, and found in it a considerable approximation to what I wanted. Much, if not most, of the philosophy of the work appeared open to objection; but the materials were there, for my own thoughts to work upon: and the author had given to those materials that first degree of elaboration, which so greatly facilitates and abridges the subsequent labour. I had now obtained what I had been waiting for. Under the impulse given me by the thoughts excited by Dr. Whewell, I read again Sir J. Herschel's Discourse on the Study of Natural Philosophy: and I was able to measure the progress my mind had made, by the great help I now found in this work — though I had read and even reviewed it several years before with little profit. I now set myself vigourously to work out the subject in thought and in writing. The time I bestowed on this had to be stolen from occupations more urgent. I had just two months to spare, at this period, in the intervals of writing for the Review. In these two months I completed the first draft of about a third, the most difficult third, of the book. What I had before written, I estimate at another third, so that only one-third remained. What I wrote at this time consisted of the remainder of the doctrine of Reasoning (the theory of Trains of Reasoning, and Demonstrative Science), and the greater part of the Book on Induction. When this was done, I had, as it seemed to me, untied all the really hard knots, and the completion of the book had become only a question of time. Having got thus far, I had to leave off in order to write two articles for the next number of the Review. When these were written, I returned to the subject, and now for the first time fell in with Comte's Cours de Philosophie Positive, or rather with the two volumes of it which were all that had at that time been published.

My theory of Induction was substantially completed before I knew of Comte's book; and it is perhaps well that I came to it by a different road from his, since the consequence has been that my treatise contains, what his certainly does not, a reduction of the inductive process to strict rules and to a scientific test, such as the Syllogism is for ratiocination. Comte is always precise and profound on the methods of investigation, but he does not even attempt any exact definition of the conditions of proof: and his writings show that he never attained a just conception of them. This, however, was specifically the problem which, in treating of Induction, I had proposed to myself. Nevertheless, I gained much from Comte, with which to enrich my chapters in the subsequent rewriting: and his book was of essential service to me in some of the parts which still remained to be thought out. As his subsequent volumes successively made their appearance, I read them with avidity, but, when he reached the subject of Social Science, with varying feelings. The fourth volume disappointed me: it contained those of his opinions on social subjects with which I most disagree. But the fifth, containing the connected view of history, rekindled all my enthusiasm; which the sixth (or concluding) volume did not materially abate. In a merely logical point of view, the only leading conception for which I am indebted to him is that of the Inverse Deductive Method, as the one chiefly applicable to the complicated subjects of History and Statistics: a process differing from the more common form of the Deductive Method in this — that instead of arriving at its conclusions by general reasoning, and verifying them by specific experience (as is the natural order in the deductive branches of physical science), it obtains its generalizations by a collation of specific experience, and verifies them by ascertaining whether they are such as would follow from known general principles. This was an idea entirely new to me when I found it in Comte: and but for him I might not soon (if ever) have arrived at it.

I had been long an ardent admirer of Comte's writings before I had any communication with himself; nor did I ever, to the last, see him in the body. But for some years we were frequent correspondents, until our correspondence became controversial, and our zeal cooled. I was the first to slacken correspondence; he was the first to drop it. I found, and he probably found likewise, that I could do no good to his mind, and that all the good he could do to mine, he did by his books. This would never have led to discontinuance of intercourse, if the differences between us had been on matters of simple doctrine. But they were chiefly on those points of opinion which blended in both of us with our strongest feelings, and determined the entire direction of our aspirations. I had fully agreed with him when he maintained that the mass of mankind, including even their rulers in all the practical departments of life, must, from the necessity of the case, accept most of their opinions on political and social matters, as they do on physical, from the authority of those who have bestowed more study on those subjects than they generally have it in their power to do. This lesson had been strongly impressed on me by the early work of Comte, to which I have adverted. And there was nothing in his great Treatise which I admired more than his remarkable exposition of the benefits which the nations of modern Europe have historically derived from the separation, during the middle ages, of temporal and spiritual power, and the distinct organization of the latter. I agreed with him that the moral and intellectual ascendancy, once exercised by priests, must in time pass into the hands of philosophers, and will naturally do so when they become sufficiently unanimous, and in other respects worthy to possess it. But when he exaggerated this line of thought into a practical system, in which philosophers were to be organized into a kind of corporate hierarchy, invested with almost the same spiritual supremacy (though without any secular power) once possessed by the Catholic church; when I found him relying on this spiritual authority as the only security for good government, the sole bulwark against practical oppression, and expecting that by it a system of despotism in the state and despotism in the family would be rendered innocuous and beneficial; it is not surprising, that while as logicians we were nearly at one, as sociologists we could travel together no further. M. Comte lived to carry out these doctrines to their extremest consequences, by planning, in his last work, the "Système de Politique Positive," the completest system of spiritual and temporal despotism which ever yet emanated from a human brain, unless possibly that of Ignatius Loyola: a system by which the yoke of general opinion, wielded by an organized body of spiritual teachers and rulers, would be made supreme over every action, and as far as is in human possibility, every thought, of every member of the community, as well in the things which regard only himself, as in those which concern the interests of others. It is but just to say that this work is a considerable improvement, in many points of feeling, over Comte's previous writings on the same subjects: but as an accession to social philosophy, the only value it seems to me to possess, consists in putting an end to the notion that no effectual moral authority can be maintained over society without the aid of religious belief; for Comte's work recognises no religion except that of Humanity, yet it leaves an irresistible conviction that any moral beliefs concurred in by the community generally, may be brought to bear upon the whole conduct and lives of its individual members, with an energy and potency truly alarming to think of. The book stands a monumental warning to thinkers on society and politics, of what happens when once men lose sight in their speculations, of the value of Liberty and of Individuality.

To return to myself. The Review engrossed, for some time longer, nearly all the time I could devote to authorship, or to thinking with authorship in view. The articles from the London and Westminster Review which are reprinted in the "Dissertations," are scarcely a fourth part of those I wrote. In the conduct of the Review I had two principal objects. One was to free philosophic radicalism from the reproach of sectarian Benthamism. I desired, while retaining the precision of expression, the definiteness

of meaning, the contempt of declamatory phrases and
vague generalities, which were so honourably characteristic
both of Bentham and of my father, to give a wider basis and
a more free and genial character to Radical speculations; to
show that there was a Radical philosophy, better and more
complete than Bentham's, while recognizing and incorporating all of Bentham's which is permanently valuable.
In this first object I, to a certain extent, succeeded. The
other thing I attempted, was to stir up the educated Radicals, in and out of Parliament, to exertion, and induce them
to make themselves, what I thought by using the proper
means they might become — a powerful party capable of
taking the government of the country, or at least of dictat-
ing the terms on which they should share it with the Whigs.
This attempt was from the first chimerical: partly because
the time was unpropitious, the Reform fervour being in its
period of ebb, and the Tory influences powerfully rallying;
but still more, because, as Austin so truly said, "the country
did not contain the men." Among the Radicals in Parliament there were several qualified to be useful members of
an enlightened Radical party, but none capable of forming
and leading such a party. The exhortations I addressed
to them found no response. One occasion did present itself
when there seemed to be room for a bold and successful
stroke for Radicalism. Lord Durham had left the ministry, by reason, as was thought, of their not being sufficiently
liberal; he afterwards accepted from them the task of ascertaining and removing the causes of the Canadian rebellion;
he had shown a disposition to surround himself at the outset
with Radical advisers; one of his earliest measures, a good
measure both in intention and in effect, having been dis-
approved and reversed by the Government at home, he had
resigned his post, and placed himself openly in a position
of quarrel with the ministers. Here was a possible chief
for a Radical party in the person of a man of importance,
who was hated by the Tories and had just been injured by

the Whigs. Any one who had the most elementary notions of party tactics, must have attempted to make something of such an opportunity. Lord Durham was bitterly attacked from all sides, inveighed against by enemies, given up by timid friends; while those who would willingly have defended him did not know what to say. He appeared to be returning a defeated and discredited man. I had followed the Canadian events from the beginning; I had been one of the prompters of his prompters; his policy was almost exactly what mine would have been, and I was in a position to defend it. I wrote and published a manifesto in the Review, in which I took the very highest ground in his behalf, claiming for him not mere acquittal, but praise and honour. Instantly a number of other writers took up the tone: I believe there was a portion of truth in what Lord Durham, soon after, with polite exaggeration, said to me — that to this article might be ascribed the almost triumphal reception which he met with on his arrival in England. I believe it to have been the word in season, which, at a critical moment, does much to decide the result; the touch which determines whether a stone, set in motion at the top of an eminence, shall roll down on one side or on the other. All hopes connected with Lord Durham as a politician soon vanished; but with regard to Canadian, and generally to colonial policy, the cause was gained: Lord Durham's report, written by Charles Buller, partly under the inspiration of Wakefield, began a new era; its recommendations, extending to complete internal self-government, were in full operation in Canada within two or three years, and have been since extended to nearly all the other colonies, of European race, which have any claim to the character of important communities. And I may say that in successfully upholding the reputation of Lord Durham and his advisers at the most important moment, I contributed materially to this result.

One other case occurred during my conduct of the

Review, which similarly illustrated the effect of taking a prompt initiative. I believe that the early success and reputation of Carlyle's French Revolution, were considerably accelerated by what I wrote about it in the Review. Immediately on its publication, and before the commonplace critics, all whose rules and modes of judgment it set at defiance, had time to pre-occupy the public with their disapproval of it, I wrote and published a review of the book, hailing it as one of those productions of genius which are above all rules, and are a law to themselves. Neither in this case nor in that of Lord Durham do I ascribe the impression, which I think was produced by what I wrote, to any particular merit of execution: indeed, in at least one of the cases (the article on Carlyle) I do not think the execution was good. And in both instances, I am persuaded that anybody, in a position to be read, who had expressed the same opinion at the same precise time, and had made any tolerable statement of the just grounds for it, would have produced the same effects. But, after the complete failure of my hopes of putting a new life into radical politics by means of the Review, I am glad to look back on these two instances of success in an honest attempt to do immediate service to things and persons that deserved it.

After the last hope of the formation of a Radical party had disappeared, it was time for me to stop the heavy expenditure of time and money which the Review cost me. It had to some extent answered my personal purpose as a vehicle for my opinions. It had enabled me to express in print much of my altered mode of thought, and to separate myself in a marked manner from the narrower Benthamism of my early writings. This was done by the general tone of all I wrote, including various purely literary articles, but especially by the two papers (reprinted in the Dissertations) which attempted a philosophical estimate of Bentham and of Coleridge. In the first of these, while doing full justice to the merits of Bentham, I pointed out what I thought the errors and deficiencies of his philosophy. The substance of this criticism I still think perfectly just; but I have sometimes doubted whether it was right to publish it at that time. I have often felt that Bentham's philosophy, as an instrument of progress, has been to some extent discredited before it had done its work, and that to lend a hand towards lowering its reputation was doing more harm than service to improvement. Now, however, when a counter-reaction appears to be setting in towards what is good in Benthamism, I can look with more satisfaction on this criticism of its defects, especially as I have myself balanced it by vindications of the fundamental principles of Bentham's philosophy, which are reprinted along with it in the same collection. In the essay on Coleridge I attempted to characterize the European reaction against the negative philosophy of the eighteenth century: and here, if the effect only of this one paper were to be considered, I might be thought to have erred by giving undue prominence to the favourable side, as I had done in the case of Bentham to the unfavourable. In both cases, the impetus with which I had detached myself from what was untenable in the doctrines of Bentham and of the eighteenth century, may have carried me, though in appearance rather than in reality, too far on the contrary side. But as far as relates to the article on Coleridge, my defence is, that I was writing for Radicals and Liberals, and it was my business to dwell most on that in writers of a different school, from the knowledge of which they might derive most improvement.

The number of the Review which contained the paper on Coleridge, was the last which was published during my proprietorship. In the spring of 1840 I made over the Review to Mr. Hickson, who had been a frequent and very useful unpaid contributor under my management: only stipulating that the change should be marked by a resumption of the old name, that of Westminster Review. Under that name Mr. Hickson conducted it for ten years, on the plan of dividing among contributors only the net proceeds of the Review, giving his own labour as writer and editor gratuitously. Under the difficulty in obtaining writers, which arose from this low scale of payment, it is highly creditable to him that he was able to maintain, in some tolerable degree, the character of the Review as an organ of radicalism and progress. I did not cease altogether to write for the Review, but continued to send it occasional contributions, not, however, exclusively; for the greater circulation of the Edinburgh Review induced me from this time to offer articles to it also when I had anything to say for which it appeared to be a suitable vehicle. And the concluding volumes of "Democracy in America," having just then come out, I inaugurated myself as a contributor to the Edinburgh, by the article on that work, which heads the second volume of the "Dissertations."

CHAPTER VII

GENERAL VIEW OF THE REMAINDER OF MY
LIFE.

FROM this time, what is worth relating of my life will come into a very small compass; for I have no further mental changes to tell of, but only, as I hope, a continued mental progress; which does not admit of a consecutive history, and the results of which, if real, will be best found in my writings. I shall, therefore, greatly abridge the chronicle of my subsequent years.

The first use I made of the leisure which I gained by disconnecting myself from the Review, was to finish the Logic. In July and August, 1838, I had found an interval in which to execute what was still undone of the original draft of the Third Book. In working out the logical theory of those laws of nature which are not laws of Causation, nor corollaries from such laws, I was led to recognize kinds as realities in nature, and not mere distinctions for convenience; a light which I had not obtained when the First Book was written, and which made it necessary for me to modify and enlarge several chapters of that Book. The Book on Language and Classification, and the chapter on the Classification of Fallacies, were drafted in the autumn of the same year; the remainder of the work, in the summer and autumn of 1840. From April following to the end of 1841, my spare time was devoted to a complete re-writing of the book from its commencement. It is in this way that all my books have been composed. They were always written at least twice over; a first draft of the entire work was completed to the very end of the subject, then the whole begun again *de novo*; but incorporating, in the second writing, all sentences and parts of sentences of the old draft, which appeared as suitable to my purpose as anything which I could write in lieu of them. I have found great advantages in this system of double redaction. It combines, better than any other mode of composition, the freshness and vigour of the first conception, with the superior precision and completeness resulting from prolonged thought. In my own case, moreover, I have found that the patience necessary for a careful elaboration of the details of composition and expression, costs much less effort after the entire subject has been once gone through, and the substance of all that I find to say has in some manner, however imperfect, been got upon paper. The only thing which I am careful, in the first draft, to make as perfect as I am able, is the arrangement. If that is bad, the whole thread on which the ideas string themselves becomes twisted; thoughts placed in a wrong connexion are not expounded in a manner that suits the right, and a first draft with this original vice is next to useless as a foundation for the final treatment.

During the re-writing of the Logic, Dr. Whewell's Philosophy of the Inductive Sciences made its appearance; a circumstance fortunate for me, as it gave me what I greatly desired, a full treatment of the subject by an antagonist, and enabled me to present my ideas with greater clearness and emphasis as well as fuller and more varied development, in defending them against definite objections, or confronting them distinctly with an opposite theory. The controversies with Dr. Whewell, as well as much matter derived from Comte, were first introduced into the book in the course of the re-writing.

At the end of 1841, the book being ready for the press, I offered it to Murray, who kept it until too late for publication that season, and then refused it, for reasons which could just as well have been given at first. But I have had no cause to regret a rejection which led to my offering it to Mr. Parker, by whom it was published in the spring of 1843. My original expectations of success were extremely limited. Archbishop Whately had, indeed, rehabilitated the name of Logic, and the study of the forms, rules, and fallacies of Ratiocination; and Dr. Whewell's writings had begun to excite an interest in the other part of my subject, the theory of Induction. A treatise, however, on a matter so abstract, could not be expected to be popular; it could only be a book for students, and students on such subjects were not only (at least in England) few, but addicted chiefly to the opposite school of metaphysics, the ontological and "innate principles" school. I therefore did not expect that the book would have many readers, or approvers; and looked for little practical effect from it, save that of keeping the tradition unbroken of what I thought a better philosophy. What hopes I had of exciting any immediate attention, were mainly grounded on the polemical propensities of Dr. Whewell; who, I thought, from observation of his conduct in other cases, would probably do something to bring the book into notice, by replying, and that promptly, to the attack on his opinions. He did reply, but not till 1850, just in time for me to answer him in the third edition. How the book came to have, for a work of the kind, so much success, and what sort of persons compose the bulk of those who have bought, I will not venture to say read, it, I have never thoroughly understood. But taken in conjunction with the many proofs which have since been given of a revival of speculation, speculation too of a free kind, in many quarters, and above all (where at one time I should have least expected it) in the Universities, the fact becomes partially intelligible. I have never indulged the illusion that the book had made any considerable impression on philosophical opinion. The German, or *à priori* view of human knowledge, and of the knowing faculties, is likely for some time longer (though it may be hoped in a diminishing degree) to predominate among those who occupy themselves with such inquiries, both here and on the Continent. But the " System of Logic " supplies what was much wanted, a text-book of the opposite doctrine — that which derives all knowledge from experience, and all moral and intellectual qualities principally from the direction given to the associations. I make as humble an estimate as anybody of what either an analysis of logical processes, or any possible canons of evidence, can do by themselves, towards guiding or rectifying the operations of the understanding. Combined with other requisites, I certainly do think them of great use; but whatever may be the practical value of a true philosophy of these matters, it is hardly possible to exaggerate the mischiefs of a false one. The notion that truths external to the mind may be known by intuition or consciousness, independently of observation and experience, is, I am persuaded, in these times, the great intellectual support of false doctrines and bad institutions. By the aid of this theory, every inveterate belief and every intense feeling, of which the origin is not remembered, is enabled to dispense with the obligation of justifying itself by reason, and is erected into its own all-sufficient voucher and justification. There never was such an instrument devised for consecrating all deep-seated prejudices. And the chief strength of this false philosophy in morals, politics, and religion, lies in the appeal which it is accustomed to make to the evidence of mathematics and of the cognate branches of physical science. To expel it from these, is to drive it from its stronghold: and because this had never been effectually done, the intuitive school, even after what my father had written in his Analysis of the Mind, had in appearance, and as far as published writings were concerned, on the whole the best of the argument. In attempting to clear up the real nature of the evidence of mathematical and physical truths, the " System of Logic " met the intuitive philosophers on ground on which they had previously been deemed unassailable; and gave its own explanation, from experience and association, of that peculiar character of what are called necessary truths, which is adduced as proof that their evidence must come from a deeper source than experience. Whether this has been done effectually, is still *sub judice;* and even then, to deprive a mode of thought so strongly rooted in human prejudices and partialities, of its mere speculative support, goes but a very little way towards overcoming it; but though only a step, it is a quite indispensable one; for since, after all, prejudice can only be successfully combated by philosophy, no way can really be made against it permanently until it has been shown not to have philosophy on its side.

Being now released from any active concern in temporary politics, and from any literary occupation involving personal communication with contributors and others, I was enabled to indulge the inclination, natural to thinking persons when the age of boyish vanity is once past, for limiting my own society to a very few persons. General society, as now carried on in England, is so insipid an affair, even to the persons who make it what it is, that it is kept up for any reason rather than the pleasure it affords. All serious discussion on matters on which opinions differ, being considered ill-bred, and the national deficiency in liveliness and sociability having prevented the cultivation of the art of talking agreeably on trifles, in which the French of the last century so much excelled, the sole attraction of what is called society to those who are not at the top of the tree, is the hope of being aided to climb a little higher in it; while to those who are already at the top, it is chiefly a compliance with custom, and with the supposed requirements of their station. To a person of any but a very common order in thought or feeling, such society, unless he has personal objects to serve by it, must be supremely unattractive: and most people, in the present day, of any really high class of intellect, make their contact with it so slight, and at such

long intervals, as to be almost considered as retiring from
it altogether.   Those persons of any mental superiority who
do   otherwise,   are,   almost   without   exception,   greatly
deteriorated by it.   Not to mention loss of time, the tone
of their feelings is lowered: they become less in earnest
about those of their opinions respecting which they must
remain silent in the society they frequent: they come to
look upon their most elevated objects as unpractical, or, at
least, too remote from realization to be more than a vision,
or a theory; and if, more fortunate than most, they retain
their higher principles unimpaired, yet with respect to the
persons and affairs of their own day they insensibly adopt
the modes of feeling and judgment in which they can hope
for sympathy from the company they keep.   A person of
high intellect should never go into unintellectual society
unless he can enter it as an apostle; yet he is the only person
with high objects who can safely enter it at all.   Persons
even of intellectual aspirations had much better, if they can,
make their habitual associates of at least their equals, and,
as far as possible, their superiors, in knowledge, intellect,
and elevation of sentiment.   Moreover, if the character is
formed, and the mind made up, on the few cardinal points
of human opinion, agreement of conviction and feeling on
these, has been felt in all times to be an essential requisite
of anything worthy the name of friendship, in a really
earnest mind.   All these circumstances united, made the
number very small of those whose society, and still more
whose intimacy, I now voluntarily sought.

Among these, by far the principal was the incomparable
friend of whom I have already spoken.   At this period she
lived mostly with one young daughter, in a quiet part of
the country, and only occasionally in town, with her first
husband, Mr. Taylor.   I visited her equally in both places;
and was greatly indebted to the strength of character which
enabled her to disregard the false interpretations liable to
be put on the frequency of my visits to her while living

generally apart from Mr. Taylor, and on our occasionally travelling together, though in all other respects our conduct during those years gave not the slightest ground for any other supposition than the true one, that our relation to each other at that time was one of strong affection and confidential intimacy only. For though we did not consider the ordinances of society binding on a subject so entirely personal, we did feel bound that our conduct should be such as in no degree to bring discredit on her husband, nor therefore on herself.

In this third period (as it may be termed) of my mental progress, which now went hand in hand with hers, my opinions gained equally in breadth and depth, I understood more things, and those which I had understood before, I now understood more thoroughly. I had now completely turned back from what there had been of excess in my reaction against Benthamism. I had, at the height of that reaction, certainly become much more indulgent to the common opinions of society and the world, and more willing to be content with seconding the superficial improvement which had begun to take place in those common opinions, than became one whose convictions on so many points, differed fundamentally from them. I was much more inclined, than I can now approve, to put in abeyance the more decidedly heretical part of my opinions, which I now look upon as almost the only ones, the assertion of which tends in any way to regenerate society. But in addition to this, our opinions were far *more* heretical than mine had been in the days of my most extreme Benthamism. In those days I had seen little further than the old school of political economists into the possibilities of fundamental improvement in social arrangements. Private property, as now understood, and inheritance, appeared to me, as to them, the *dernier mot* of legislation: and I looked no further than to mitigating the inequalities consequent on these institutions, by getting rid of primogeniture and entails. The notion that it was possible to go further than this in removing the injustice — for injustice it is, whether admitting of a complete remedy or not — involved in the fact that some are born to riches and the vast majority to poverty, I then reckoned chimerical, and only hoped that by universal education, leading to voluntary restraint on population, the portion of the poor might be made more tolerable. In short, I was a democrat, but not the least of a Socialist. We were now much less democrats than I had been, because so long as education continues to be so wretchedly imperfect, we dreaded the ignorance and especially the selfishness and brutality of the mass: but our ideal of ultimate improvement went far beyond Democracy, and would class us decidedly under the general designation of Socialists. While we repudiated with the greatest energy that tyranny of society over the individual which most Socialistic systems are supposed to involve, we yet looked forward to a time when society will no longer be divided into the idle and the industrious; when the rule that they who do not work shall not eat, will be applied not to paupers only, but impartially to all; when the division of the produce of labour, instead of depending, as in so great a degree it now does, on the accident of birth, will be made by concert on an acknowledged principle of justice; and when it will no longer either be, or be thought to be, impossible for human beings to exert themselves strenuously in procuring benefits which are not to be exclusively their own, but to be shared with the society they belong to. The social problem of the future we considered to be, how to unite the greatest individual liberty of action, with a common ownership in the raw material of the globe, and an equal participation of all in the benefits of combined labour. We had not the presumption to suppose that we could already foresee, by what precise form of institutions these objects could most effectually be attained, or at how near or how distant a period they would become practicable. We saw clearly that to render any such social transformation either possible or desirable, an equivalent change of character must take place both in the uncultivated herd who now compose the labouring masses, and in the immense majority of their employers. Both these classes must learn by practice to labour and combine for generous, or at all events for public and social purposes, and not, as hitherto, solely for narrowly interested ones. But the capacity to do this has always existed in mankind, and is not, nor is ever likely to be, extinct. Education, habit, and the cultivation of the sentiments, will make a common man dig or weave for his country, as readily as fight for his country. True enough, it is only by slow degrees, and a system of culture prolonged through successive generations, that men in general can be brought up to this point. But the hindrance is not in the essential constitution of human nature. Interest in the common good is at present so weak a motive in the generality, not because it can never be otherwise, but because the mind is not accustomed to dwell on it as it dwells from morning till night on things which tend only to personal advantage. When called into activity, as only self-interest now is, by the daily course of life, and spurred from behind by the love of distinction and the fear of shame, it is capable of producing, even in common men, the most strenuous exertions as well as the most heroic sacrifices. The deep-rooted selfishness which forms the general character of the existing state of society, is *so* deeply rooted, only because the whole course of existing institutions tends to foster it; modern institutions in some respects more than ancient, since the occasions on which the individual is called on to do anything for the public without receiving its pay, are far less frequent in modern life, than in the smaller commonwealths of antiquity. These considerations did not make us overlook the folly of premature attempts to dispense with the inducements of private interest in social affairs, while no substitute for them has been or can be provided: but we regarded all existing institutions and social arrangements as being (in a phrase I once heard from Austin) " merely provisional," and we welcomed with the greatest pleasure and interest all socialistic experiments by select individuals (such as the Co-operative Societies), which, whether they succeeded or failed, could not but operate as a most useful education of those who took part in them, by cultivating their capacity of acting upon motives pointing directly to the general good, or making them aware of the defects which render them and others incapable of doing so.

In the " Principles of Political Economy," these opinions were promulgated, less clearly and fully in the first edition, rather more so in the second, and quite unequivocally in the third. The difference arose partly from the change of times, the first edition having been written and sent to press before the French Revolution of 1848, after which the public mind became more open to the reception of novelties in opinion, and doctrines appeared moderate which would have been thought very startling a short time before. In the first edition the difficulties of Socialism were stated so strongly, that the tone was on the whole that of opposition to it. In the year or two which followed, much time was given to the study of the best Socialistic writers on the Continent, and to meditation and discussion on the whole range of topics involved in the controversy: and the result was that most of what had been written on the subject in the first edition was cancelled, and replaced by arguments and reflections which represent a more advanced opinion.

The Political Economy was far more rapidly executed than the Logic, or indeed than anything of importance which I had previously written. It was commenced in the autumn of 1845, and was ready for the press before the end of 1847. In this period of little more than two years there was an interval of six months during which the work was laid aside, while I was writing articles in the Morning Chronicle (which unexpectedly entered warmly into my purpose) urging the formation of peasant properties on the waste lands of Ireland. This was during the period of the Famine, the winter of 1846–47, when the stern necessities of the time seemed to afford a chance of gaining attention for what appeared to me the only mode of combining relief to immediate destitution with permanent improvement of the social and economical condition of the Irish people. But the idea was new and strange; there was no English precedent for such a proceeding: and the profound ignorance of English politicians and the English public concerning all social phenomena not generally met with in England (however common elsewhere), made my endeavours an entire failure. Instead of a great operation on the waste lands, and the conversion of cottiers into proprietors, Parliament passed a Poor Law for maintaining them as paupers: and if the nation has not since found itself in inextricable difficulties from the joint operation of the old evils and the quack remedy, it is indebted for its deliverance to that most unexpected and surprising fact, the depopulation of Ireland, commenced by famine, and continued by emigration.

The rapid success of the Political Economy showed that the public wanted, and were prepared for such a book. Published early in 1848, an edition of a thousand copies was sold in less than a year. Another similar edition was published in the spring of 1849; and a third, of 1250 copies, early in 1852. It was, from the first, continually cited and referred to as an authority, because it was not a book merely of abstract science, but also of application, and treated Political Economy not as a thing by itself, but as a fragment of a greater whole; a branch of Social Philosophy, so interlinked with all the other branches, that its conclusions, even in its own peculiar province, are only true conditionally, subject to interference and counteraction from causes not directly within its scope: while to the character of a practical guide it has no pretension, apart from other classes of considerations. Political Economy, in truth, has never pretended to give advice to mankind with no lights but its own; though people who knew nothing but political economy (and therefore knew that ill) have taken upon themselves to advise, and could only do so by such lights as they had. But the numerous sentimental enemies of political economy, and its still more numerous interested enemies in sentimental guise, have been very successful in gaining belief for this among other unmerited imputations against it, and the "Principles" having, in spite of the freedom of many of its opinions, become for the present the most popular treatise on the subject, has helped to disarm the enemies of so important a study. The amount of its worth as an exposition of the science, and the value of the different applications which it suggests, others of course must judge.

For a considerable time after this, I published no work of magnitude; though I still occasionally wrote in periodicals, and my correspondence (much of it with persons quite unknown to me), on subjects of public interest, swelled to a considerable bulk. During these years I wrote or commenced various Essays, for eventual publication, on some of the fundamental questions of human and social life, with regard to several of which I have already much exceeded the severity of the Horatian precept. I continued to watch with keen interest the progress of public events. But it was not, on the whole, very encouraging to me. The European reaction after 1848, and the success of an unprincipled usurper in December, 1851, put an end, as it seemed, to all present hope for freedom or social improvement in France and the Continent. In England, I had seen and continued to see many of the opinions of my youth obtain general recognition, and many of the reforms in institutions, for which I had through life contended, either

effected or in course of being so. But these changes had
been attended with much less benefit to human well-being
than I should formerly have anticipated, because they had
produced very little improvement in that which all real
amelioration in the lot of mankind depends on, their
intellectual and moral state: and it might even be questioned
if the various causes of deterioration which had been at
work in the meanwhile, had not more than counterbalanced
the tendencies to improvement. I had learnt from experience that many false opinions may be exchanged for true
ones, without in the least altering the habits of mind of
which false opinions are the result. The English public,
for example, are quite as raw and undiscerning on subjects
of political economy since the nation has been converted to
free-trade, as they were before; and are still further from
having acquired better habits of thought and feeling, or
being in any way better fortified against error, on subjects
of a more elevated character. For, though they have
thrown off certain errors, the general discipline of their
minds, intellectually and morally, is not altered. I am
now convinced, that no great improvements in the lot of
mankind are possible, until a great change takes place in
the fundamental constitution of their modes of thought.
The old opinions in religion, morals, and politics, are so
much discredited in the more intellectual minds as to have
lost the greater part of their efficacy for good, while they
have still life enough in them to be a powerful obstacle to
the growing up of any better opinions on those subjects.
When the philosophic minds of the world can no longer
believe its religion, or can only believe it with modifications
amounting to an essential change of its character, a tran-
sitional period commences, of weak convictions, paralysed
intellects, and growing laxity of principle, which cannot
terminate until a renovation has been effected in the basis
of their belief leading to the elevation of some faith,
whether religious or merely human, which they can really

believe: and when things are in this state, all thinking or writing which does not tend to promote such a renovation, is of very little value beyond the moment. Since there was little in the apparent condition of the public mind, indicative of any tendency in this direction, my view of the immediate prospects of human improvement was not sanguine. More recently a spirit of free speculation has sprung up, giving a more encouraging prospect of the gradual mental emancipation of England; and concurring with the renewal under better auspices, of the movement for political freedom in the rest of Europe, has given to the present condition of human affairs a more hopeful aspect.[1]

Between the time of which I have now spoken, and the present, took place the most important events of my private life. The first of these was my marriage, in April, 1851, to the lady whose incomparable worth had made her friendship the greatest source to me both of happiness and of improvement, during many years in which we never expected to be in any closer relation to one another. Ardently as I should have aspired to this complete union of our lives at any time in the course of my existence at which it had been practicable, I, as much as my wife, would far rather have foregone that privilege for ever, than have owed it to the premature death of one for whom I had the sincerest respect, and she the strongest affection. That event, however, having taken place in July, 1849, it was granted to me to derive from that evil my own greatest good, by adding to the partnership of thought, feeling, and writing which had long existed, a partnership of our entire existence. For seven and a half years that blessing was mine; for seven and a half only! I can say nothing which could describe, even in the faintest manner, what that loss was and is. But because I know that she would have wished it, I endeavour to make the best of what life I have left, and

---

[1] Note in edition of 1873, " written about 1861."

to work on for her purposes with such diminished strength as can be derived from thoughts of her, and communion with her memory.

During the years which intervened between the commencement of my married life and the catastrophe which closed it, the principal occurrences of my outward existence (unless I count as such a first attack of the family disease, and a consequent journey of more than six months for the recovery of health, in Italy, Sicily, and Greece) had reference to my position in the India House. In 1856 I was promoted to the rank of chief of the office in which I had served for upwards of thirty-three years. The appointment, that of Examiner of India Correspondence, was the highest, next to that of Secretary, in the East India Company's home service, involving the general superintendence of all the correspondence with the Indian Governments, except the military, naval, and financial. I held this office as long as it continued to exist, being a little more than two years; after which it pleased Parliament, in other words Lord Palmerston, to put an end to the East India Company as a branch of the government of India under the Crown, and convert the administration of that country into a thing to be scrambled for by the second and third class of English parliamentary politicians. I was the chief manager of the resistance which the Company made to their own political extinction. To the letters and petitions I wrote for them, and the concluding chapter of my treatise on Representative Government, I must refer for my opinions on the folly and mischief of this ill-considered change. Personally I considered myself a gainer by it, as I had given enough of my life to India, and was not unwilling to retire on the liberal compensation granted. After the change was consummated, Lord Stanley, the first Secretary of State for India, made me the honourable offer of a seat in the Council, and the proposal was subsequently renewed by the Council itself, on the first occasion of its having to

supply a vacancy in its own body. But the conditions of
Indian government under the new system made me antici-
pate nothing but useless vexation and waste of effort from
any participation in it: and nothing that has since happened
has had any tendency to make me regret my refusal.

During the two years which immediately preceded the
cessation of my official life, my wife and I were working
together at the " Liberty." I had first planned and written
it as a short essay in 1854. It was in mounting the steps
of the Capitol, in January, 1855, that the thought first
arose of converting it into a volume. None of my writings
have been either so carefully composed, or so sedulously
corrected as this. After it had been written as usual twice
over, we kept it by us, bringing it out from time to time,
and going through it *de novo*, reading, weighing, and
criticizing every sentence. Its final revision was to have
been a work of the winter of 1858-9, the first after my
retirement, which we had arranged to pass in the South of
Europe. That hope and every other were frustrated by
the most unexpected and bitter calamity of her death — at
Avignon, on our way to Montpellier, from a sudden attack
of pulmonary congestion.

Since then I have sought for such alleviation as my state
admitted of, by the mode of life which most enabled me
to feel her still near me. I bought a cottage as close as
possible to the place where she is buried, and there her
daughter (my fellow-sufferer and now my chief comfort)
and I, live constantly during a great portion of the year.
My objects in life are solely those which were hers; my
pursuits and occupations those in which she shared, or
sympathized, and which are indissolubly associated with her.
Her memory is to me a religion, and her approbation the
standard by which, summing up as it does all worthiness,
I endeavour to regulate my life.

In resuming my pen some years after closing the preceding narrative, I am influenced by a desire not to have

incomplete the record, for the sake of which chiefly this
biographical sketch was undertaken, of the obligations I
owe to those who have either contributed essentially to my
own mental development or had a direct share in my writings and in whatever else of a public nature I have done.
In the preceding pages, this record, so far as it relates to
my wife, is not so detailed and precise as it ought to be;
and since I lost her, I have had other help, not less deserving and requiring acknowledgment.

When two persons have their thoughts and speculations
completely in common; when all subjects of intellectual
or moral interest are discussed between them in daily life,
and probed to much greater depths than are usually or con-
veniently sounded in writings intended for general readers;
when they set out from the same principles, and arrive at
their conclusions by processes pursued jointly, it is of little
consequence in respect to the question of originality, which
of them holds the pen; the one who contributes least to the
composition may contribute most to the thought; the writings which result are the joint product of both, and it must
often be impossible to disentangle their respective parts,
and affirm that this belongs to one and that to the other.
In this wide sense, not only during the years of our married
life, but during many of the years of confidential friendship
which preceded it, all my published writings were as much
my wife's work as mine; her share in them constantly increasing as years advanced. But in certain cases, what
belongs to her can be distinguished, and specially identified.
Over and above the general influence which her mind had
over mine, the most valuable ideas and features in these
joint productions — those which have been most fruitful of
important results, and have contributed most to the success
and reputation of the works themselves — originated with
her, were emanations from her mind, my part in them
being no greater than in any of the thoughts which I found
in previous writers, and made my own only by incorporating

them with my own system of thought. During the greater part of my literary life I have performed the office in relation to her, which from a rather early period I had considered as the most useful part that I was qualified to take in the domain of thought, that of an interpreter of original thinkers, and mediator between them and the public; for I had always a humble opinion of my own powers as an original thinker, except in abstract science (logic, metaphysics, and the theoretic principles of political economy and politics), but thought myself much superior to most of my contemporaries in willingness and ability to learn from everybody; as I found hardly any one who made such a point of examining what was said in defence of all opinions, however new or however old, in the conviction that even if they were errors there might be a substratum of truth underneath them, and that in any case the discovery of what it was that made them plausible, would be a benefit to truth. I had, in consequence, marked out this as a sphere of usefulness in which I was under a special obligation to make myself active: the more so, as the acquaintance I had formed with the ideas of the Coleridgians, of the German thinkers, and of Carlyle, all of them fiercely opposed to the mode of thought in which I had been brought up, had convinced me that along with much error they possessed much truth, which was veiled from minds otherwise capable of receiving it by the transcendental and mystical phraseology in which they were accustomed to shut it up, and from which they neither cared, nor knew how, to disengage it; and I did not despair of separating the truth from the error, and expressing it in terms which would be intelligible and not repulsive to those on my own side in philosophy. Thus prepared, it will easily be believed that when I came into close intellectual communion with a person of the most eminent faculties, whose genius, as it grew and unfolded itself in thought, continually struck out truths far in advance of me, but in which I could not, as I had done in those others, detect any mixture of error, the greatest part of my mental growth consisted in the assimilation of those truths, and the most valuable part of my intellectual work was in building the bridges and clearing the paths which connected them with my general system of thought.[1]

The first of my books in which her share was conspicuous was the " Principles of Political Economy." The " System of Logic " owed little to her except in the minuter matters of composition, in which respect my writings, both great and small, have largely benefited by her accurate and clear-

---

[1] The steps in my mental growth for which I was indebted to her were far from being those which a person wholly uninformed on the subject would probably suspect. It might be supposed, for instance, that my strong convictions on the complete equality in all legal, political, social and domestic relations, which ought to exist between men and women, may have been adopted or learnt from her. This was so far from being the fact, that those convictions were among the earliest results of the application of my mind to political subjects, and the strength with which I held them was, as I believe, more than anything else, the originating cause of the interest she felt in me. What is true is, that until I knew her, the opinion was in my mind, little more than an abstract principle. I saw no more reason why women should be held in legal subjection to other people, than why men should. I was certain that their interests required fully as much protection as those of men, and were quite as little likely to obtain it without an equal voice in making the laws by which they are to be bound. But that perception of the vast practical bearings of women's disabilities which found expression in the book on the " Subjection of Women " was acquired mainly through her teaching. But for her rare knowledge of human nature and comprehension of moral and social influences, though I should doubtless have held my present opinions, I should have had a very insufficient perception of the mode in which the consequences of the inferior position of women intertwine themselves with all the evils of existing society and with all the difficulties of human improvement. I am indeed painfully conscious how much of her best thoughts on the subject I have failed to reproduce, and how greatly that little treatise falls short of what would have been if she had put on paper her entire mind on this question, or had lived to revise and improve, as she certainly would have done, my imperfect statement of the case.

sighted criticism.[1]   The chapter of the Political Economy which has had a greater influence on opinion than all the rest, that on "the Probable Future of the Labouring Classes," is entirely due to her: in the first draft of the book, that chapter did not exist.   She pointed out the need of such a chapter, and the extreme imperfection of the book without it: she was the cause of my writing it; and the more general part of the chapter, the statement and discussion of the two opposite theories respecting the proper condition of the labouring classes, was wholly an exposition of her thoughts, often in words taken from her own lips.   The purely scientific part of the Political Economy I did not learn from her; but it was chiefly her influence that gave to the book that general tone by which it is distinguished from all previous expositions of Political Economy that had any pretension to being scientific, and which has made it so useful in conciliating minds which those previous expositions had repelled.   This tone consisted chiefly in making the proper distinction between the laws of the Production

[1] The only person from whom I received any direct assistance in the preparation of the "System of Logic" was Mr. Bain, since so justly celebrated for his philosophical writings.   He went carefully through the manuscript before it was sent to press, and enriched it with a great number of additional examples and illustrations from science; many of which, as well as some detached remarks of his own in confirmation of my logical views, I inserted nearly in his own words.

My obligations to Comte were only to his writings — to the part which had then been published of his "Système de Philosophie Positive:" and, as has been seen from what I have said in the Narrative, the amount of these obligations is far less than has sometimes been asserted.   The first volume, which contains all the fundamental doctrines of the book, was substantially complete before I had seen Comte's treatise.   I derived from him many valuable thoughts, conspicuously in the chapter on Hypotheses and in the view taken of the logic of algebra: but it is only in the concluding Book, on the Logic of the Moral Sciences, that I owe to him any radical improvement in my conception of the application of logical methods.   This improvement I have stated and characterized in a former part of the present Memoir.

of Wealth, which are real laws of nature, dependent on the properties of objects, and the modes of its Distribution, which, subject to certain conditions, depend on human will. The common run of political economists confuse these together, under the designation of economic laws, which they deem incapable of being defeated or modified by human effort; ascribing the same necessity to things dependent on the unchangeable conditions of our earthly existence, and to those which, being but the necessary consequences of particular social arrangements, are merely co-extensive with these: given certain institutions and customs, wages, profits, and rent will be determined by certain causes; but this class of political economists drop the indispensable presupposition, and argue that these causes must, by an inherent necessity, against which no human means can avail, determine the shares which fall, in the division of the produce, to labourers, capitalists, and landlords. The " Principles of Political Economy " yielded to none of its predecessors in aiming at the scientific appreciation of the action of these causes, under the conditions which they presuppose; but it set the example of not treating those conditions as final. The economic generalizations which depend, not on necessities of nature but on those combined with the existing arrangements of society, it deals with only as provisional, and as liable to be much altered by the progress of social improvement. I had indeed partially learnt this view of things from the thoughts awakened in me by the speculations of the St. Simonians; but it was made a living principle pervading and animating the book by my wife's promptings. This example illustrates well the general character of what she contributed to my writings. What was abstract and purely scientific was generally mine; the properly human element came from her: in all that concerned the application of philosophy to the exigencies of human society and progress, I was her pupil, alike in boldness of speculation and cautiousness of practical judgment.

For, on the one hand, she was much more courageous and
far-sighted than without her I should have been, in anticipations of an order of things to come, in which many of the
limited generalizations now so often confounded with universal principles will cease to be applicable. Those parts
of my writings, and especially of the Political Economy,
which contemplate possibilities in the future such as, when
affirmed by Socialists, have in general been fiercely denied
by political economists, would, but for her, either have
been absent, or the suggestions would have been made much
more timidly and in a more qualified form. But while she
thus rendered me bolder in speculation on human affairs,
her practical turn of mind, and her almost unerring estimate of practical obstacles, repressed in me all tendencies
that were really visionary. Her mind invested all ideas in
a concrete shape, and formed to itself a conception of how
they would actually work: and her knowledge of the existing feelings and conduct of mankind was so seldom at fault,
that the weak point in any unworkable suggestion seldom
escaped her.[1]

The " Liberty " was more directly and literally our joint
production than anything else which bears my name, for
there was not a sentence of it that was not several times
gone through by us together, turned over in many ways,
and carefully weeded of any faults, either in thought or
expression, that we detected in it. It is in consequence of
this that, although it never underwent her final revision, it
far surpasses, as a mere specimen of composition, anything
which has proceeded from me either before or since. With
regard to the thoughts, it is difficult to identify any particular part or element as being more hers than all the rest.
The whole mode of thinking of which the book was the

[1] A few dedicatory lines acknowledging what the book owed to her,
were prefixed to some of the presentation copies of the Political Economy
on its first publication. Her dislike of publicity alone prevented their
insertion in the other copies of the work.

expression, was emphatically hers. But I also was so thoroughly imbued with it, that the same thoughts naturally occurred to us both. That I was thus penetrated with it, however, I owe in a great degree to her. There was a moment in my mental progress when I might easily have fallen into a tendency towards over-government, both social and political; as there was also a moment when, by reaction from a contrary excess, I might have become a less thorough radical and democrat than I am. In both these points, as in many others, she benefited me as much by keeping me right where I was right, as by leading me to new truths, and ridding me of errors. My great readiness and eagerness to learn from everybody, and to make room in my opinions for every new acquisition by adjusting the old and the new to one another, might, but for her steadying influence, have seduced me into modifying my early opinions too much. She was in nothing more valuable to my mental development than by her just measure of the relative importance of different considerations, which often protected me from allowing to truths I had only recently learnt to see, a more important place in my thoughts than was properly their due.

The " Liberty " is likely to survive longer than anything else that I have written (with the possible exception of the " Logic "), because the conjunction of her mind with mine has rendered it a kind of philosophic text-book of a single truth, which the changes progressively taking place in modern society tend to bring out into ever stronger relief: the importance, to man and society, of a large variety in types of character, and of giving full freedom to human nature to expand itself in innumerable and conflicting directions. Nothing can better show how deep are the foundations of this truth, than the great impression made by the exposition of it at a time which, to superficial observation, did not seem to stand much in need of such a lesson. The fears we expressed, lest the inevitable growth of social equality and of the government of public opinion, should impose on mankind an oppressive yoke of uniformity in opinion and practice, might easily have appeared chimerical to those who looked more at present facts than at tendencies; for the gradual revolution that is taking place in society and institutions has, thus far, been decidedly favourable to the development of new opinions, and has procured for them a much more unprejudiced hearing than they previously met with. But this is a feature belonging to periods of transition, when old notions and feelings have been unsettled, and no new doctrines have yet succeeded to their ascendancy. At such times people of any mental activity, having given up many of their old beliefs, and not feeling quite sure that those they still retain can stand unmodified, listen eagerly to new opinions. But this state of things is necessarily transitory: some particular body of doctrine in time rallies the majority round it, organizes social institutions and modes of action conformably to itself, education impresses this new creed upon the new generations without the mental processes that have led to it, and by degrees it acquires the very same power of compression, so long exercised by the creeds of which it had taken the place. Whether this noxious power will be exercised, depends on whether mankind have by that time become aware that it cannot be exercised without stunting and dwarfing human nature. It is then that the teachings of the "Liberty" will have their greatest value. And it is to be feared that they will retain that value a long time.

As regards originality, it has of course no other than that which every thoughtful mind gives to its own mode of conceiving and expressing truths which are common property. The leading thought of the book is one which though in many ages confined to insulated thinkers, mankind have probably at no time since the beginning of civilization been entirely without. To speak only of the last few generations, it is distinctly contained in the vein of important thought respecting education and culture, spread through the European mind by the labours and genius of Pestalozzi. The unqualified championship of it by Wilhelm von Humboldt is referred to in the book; but he by no means stood alone in his own country. During the early part of the present century the doctrine of the rights of individuality, and the claim of the moral nature to develop itself in its own way, was pushed by a whole school of German authors even to exaggeration; and the writings of Goethe, the most celebrated of all German authors, though not belonging to that or to any other school, are penetrated throughout by views of morals and of conduct in life, often in my opinion not defensible, but which are incessantly seeking whatever defence they admit of in the theory of the right and duty of self-development. In our own country, before the book " On Liberty " was written, the doctrine of Individuality had been enthusiastically asserted, in a style of vigorous declamation sometimes reminding one of Fichte, by Mr. William Maccall, in a series of writings of which the most elaborate is entitled " Elements of Individualism: " and a remarkable American, Mr. Warren, had framed a System of Society, on the foundation of " the Sovereignty of the Individual," had obtained a number of followers, and had actually commenced the formation of a Village Community (whether it now exists I know not), which, though bearing a superficial resemblance to some of the projects of Socialists, is diametrically opposite to them in principle, since it recognizes no authority whatever in Society over the individual, except to enforce equal freedom of development for all individualities. As the book which bears my name claimed no originality for any of its doctrines, and was not intended to write their history, the only author who had preceded me in their assertion, of whom I thought it appropriate to say anything, was Humboldt, who furnished the motto to the work; although in one passage I borrowed from the

Warrenites their phrase, the sovereignty of the individual. It is hardly necessary here to remark that there are abundant differences in detail, between the conception of the doctrine by any of the predecessors I have mentioned, and that set forth in the book.

After my irreparable loss, one of my earliest cares was to print and publish the treatise, so much of which was the work of her whom I had lost, and consecrate it to her memory. I have made no alteration or addition to it, nor shall I ever. Though it wants the last touch of her hand, no substitute for that touch shall ever be attempted by mine.

The political circumstances of the time induced me, shortly after, to complete and publish a pamphlet ("Thoughts on Parliamentary Reform"), part of which had been written some years previously, on the occasion of one of the abortive Reform Bills, and had at the time been approved and revised by her. Its principal features were, hostility to the Ballot (a change of opinion in both of us, in which she rather preceded me), and a claim of representation for minorities; not, however, at that time going beyond the cumulative vote proposed by Mr. Garth Marshall. In finishing the pamphlet for publication, with a view to the discussions on the Reform Bill of Lord Derby's and Mr. Disraeli's Government in 1859, I added a third feature, a plurality of votes, to be given, not to property, but to proved superiority of education. This recommended itself to me as a means of reconciling the irresistible claim of every man or woman to be consulted, and to be allowed a voice, in the regulation of affairs which vitally concern them, with the superiority of weight justly due to opinions grounded on superiority of knowledge. The suggestion, however, was one which I had never discussed with my almost infallible counsellor, and I have no evidence that she would have concurred in it. As far as I have been able to observe, it has found favour with nobody; all who desire any sort of inequality in the electoral vote, desiring it in favour of property and not of intelligence or knowledge. If it ever overcomes the strong feeling which exists against it, this will only be after the establishment of a systematic National Education by which the various grades of politically valuable acquirement may be accurately defined and authenticated. Without this it will always remain liable to strong, possibly conclusive, objections; and with this, it would perhaps not be needed.

It was soon after the publication of " Thoughts on Parliamentary Reform," that I became acquainted with Mr. Hare's admirable system of Personal Representation, which, in its present shape, was then for the first time published. I saw in this great practical and philosophical idea, the greatest improvement of which the system of representative government is susceptible; an improvement which, in the most felicitous manner, exactly meets and cures the grand, and what before seemed the inherent, defect of the representative system; that of giving to a numerical majority all power, instead of only a power proportional to its numbers, and enabling the strongest party to exclude all weaker parties from making their opinions heard in the assembly of the nation, except through such opportunity as may be given to them by the accidentally unequal distribution of opinions in different localities. To these great evils nothing more than very imperfect palliatives had seemed possible; but Mr. Hare's system affords a radical cure. This great discovery, for it is no less, in the political art, inspired me, as I believe it has inspired all thoughtful persons who have adopted it, with new and more sanguine hopes respecting the prospects of human society; by freeing the form of political institutions towards which the whole civilized world is manifestly and irresistibly tending, from the chief part of what seemed to qualify, or render doubtful, its ultimate benefits. Minorities, so long as they remain minorities, are, and ought to be, outvoted; but under arrangements which enable any assemblage of voters, amounting to a certain number, to place in the legislature a representative of its own choice, minorities cannot be suppressed. Independent opinions will force their way into the council of the nation and make themselves heard there, a thing which often cannot happen in the existing forms of representative democracy; and the legislature, instead of being weeded of individual peculiarities and entirely made up of men who simply represent the creed of great political or religious parties, will comprise a large proportion of the most eminent individual minds in the country, placed there, without reference to party, by voters who appreciate their individual eminence.   I can understand that persons, otherwise intelligent, should, for want of sufficient examination, be repelled from Mr. Hare's plan by what they think the complex nature of its machinery.   But any one who does not feel the want which the scheme is intended to supply; any one who throws it over as a mere theoretical subtlety or crotchet, tending to no valuable purpose, and unworthy of the attention of practical men, may be pronounced an incompetent statesman, unequal to the politics of the future. I mean, unless he is a minister or aspires to become one: for we are quite accustomed to a minister continuing to profess unqualified hostility to an improvement almost to the very day when his conscience or his interest induces him to take it up as a public measure, and carry it.

Had I met with Mr. Hare's system before the publication of my pamphlet, I should have given an account of it there. Not having done so, I wrote an article in Fraser's Magazine (reprinted in my miscellaneous writings) principally for that purpose, though I included in it, along with Mr. Hare's book, a review of two other productions on the question of the day; one of them a pamphlet by my early friend, Mr. John Austin, who had in his old age become an enemy to all further Parliamentary reform; the other an able and ingenious, though partially erroneous, work by Mr. Lorimer.

In the course of the same summer I fulfilled a duty

particularly incumbent upon me, that of helping (by an article in the Edinburgh Review) to make known Mr. Bain's profound treatise on the Mind, just then completed by the publication of its second volume. And I carried through the press a selection of my minor writings, forming the first two volumes of " Dissertations and Discussions." The selection had been made during my wife's lifetime, but the revision, in concert with her, with a view to repub- lication, had been barely commenced; and when I had no longer the guidance of her judgment I despaired of pur- suing it further, and republished the papers as they were, with the exception of striking out such passages as were no longer in accordance with my opinions. My literary work of the year was terminated with an essay in Fraser's maga- zine (afterwards republished in the third volume of " Dis- sertations and Discussions,") entitled " A Few Words on Non-Intervention." I was prompted to write this paper by a desire, while vindicating England from the imputa- tions commonly brought against her on the Continent, of a peculiar selfishness in matters of foreign policy, to warn Englishmen of the colour given to this imputation by the low tone in which English statesmen are accustomed to speak of English policy as concerned only with English interests, and by the conduct of Lord Palmerston at that particular time in opposing the Suez Canal: and I took the opportunity of expressing ideas which had long been in my mind (some of them generated by my Indian experience, and others by the international questions which then greatly occupied the European public), respecting the true prin- ciples of international morality, and the legitimate modi- fications made in it by difference of times and circumstances; a subject I had already, to some extent, discussed in the vindication of the French Provisional Government of 1848 against the attacks of Lord Brougham and others, which I published at the time in the Westminster Review, and which is reprinted in the " Dissertations."

I had now settled, as I believed, for the remainder of

my existence into a purely literary life; if that can be called literary which continued to be occupied in a pre-eminent degree with politics, and not merely with theoretical, but practical politics, although a great part of the year was spent at a distance of many hundred miles from the chief seat of the politics of my own country, to which, and primarily for which, I wrote. But, in truth, the modern facilities of communication have not only removed all the disadvantages, to a political writer in tolerably easy circumstances, of distance from the scene of political action, but have converted them into advantages. . The immediate and regular receipt of newspapers and periodicals keeps him *au courant* of even the most temporary politics, and gives him a much more correct view of the state and progress of opinion than he could acquire by personal contact with individuals: for every one's social intercourse is more or less limited to particular sets or classes, whose impressions and no others reach him through that channel; and experience has taught me that those who give their time to the absorbing claims of what is called society, not having leisure to keep up a large acquaintance with the organs of opinion, remain much more ignorant of the general state either of the public mind, or of the active and instructed part of it, than a recluse who reads the newspapers need be. There are, no doubt, disadvantages in too long a separation from one's country — in not occasionally renewing one's impressions of the light in which men and things appear when seen from a position in the midst of them; but the deliberate judgment formed at a distance, and undisturbed by inequalities of perspective, is the most to be depended on, even for application to practice. Alternating between the two positions, I combined the advantages of both. And, though the inspirer of my best thoughts was no longer with me, I was not alone: she had left a daughter, my step-daughter, Miss Helen Taylor, the inheritor of much of her wisdom, and of all her nobleness of character, whose ever growing and ripening talents from that day to this have been devoted to the same great purposes, and have already made her name better and more widely known than was that of her mother, though far less so than I predict, that if she lives it is destined to become. Of the value of her direct co-operation with me, something will be said hereafter, of what I owe in the way of instruction to her great powers of original thought and soundness of practical judgment, it would be a vain attempt to give an adequate idea. Surely no one ever before was so fortunate, as, after such a loss as mine, to draw another prize in the lottery of life — another companion, stimulator, adviser, and instructor of the rarest quality. Whoever, either now or hereafter, may think of me and of the work I have done, must never forget that it is the product not of one intellect and conscience, but of three, the least considerable of whom, and above all the least original, is the one whose name is attached to it.

The work of the years 1860 and 1861 consisted chiefly of two treatises, only one of which was intended for immediate publication. This was the " Considerations on Representative Government "; a connected exposition of what, by the thoughts of many years, I had come to regard as the best form of a popular constitution. Along with as much of the general theory of government as is necessary to support this particular portion of its practice, the volume contains my matured views of the principal questions which occupy the present age, within the province of purely organic institutions, and raises, by anticipation, some other questions to which growing necessities will sooner or later compel the attention both of theoretical and of practical politicians. The chief of these last, is the distinction between the function of making laws, for which a numerous popular assembly is radically unfit, and that of getting good laws made, which is its proper duty and cannot be satisfactorily fulfilled by any other authority: and the con-

sequent need of a Legislative Commission, as a permanent
part of the constitution of a free country; consisting of a
small number of highly trained political minds, on whom,
when Parliament has determined that a law shall be made,
the task of making it should be devolved: Parliament retaining the power of passing or rejecting the bill when
drawn up, but not of altering it otherwise than by sending
proposed amendments to be dealt with by the Commission.
The question here raised respecting the most important of
all public functions, that of legislation, is a particular case
of the great problem of modern political organization,
stated, I believe, for the first time in its full extent by
Bentham, though in my opinion not alway. satisfactorily
resolved by him; the combination of complete popular control over public affairs, with the greatest attainable perfection of skilled agency.

The other treatise written at this time is the one which
was published some years later under the title of "The
Subjection of Women." It was written at my daughter's
suggestion that there might, in any event, be in existence
a written exposition of my opinions on that great question,
as full and conclusive as I could make it. The intention
was to keep this among other unpublished papers, improving it from time to time if I was able, and to publish it at
the time when it should seem likely to be most useful. As
ultimately published it was enriched with some important
ideas of my daughter's, and passages of her writing. But
in what was of my own composition, all that is most striking
and profound belongs to my wife; coming from the fund
of thought which had been made common to us both, by
our innumerable conversations and discussions on a topic
which filled so large a place in our minds.

Soon after this time I took from their repository a portion of the unpublished papers which I had written during
the last years of our married life, and shaped them, with
some additional matter, into the little work entitled "Utili-

tarianism "; which was first published, in three parts, in successive numbers of Fraser's Magazine, and afterwards reprinted in a volume.

Before this, however, the state of public affairs had become extremely critical, by the commencement of the American civil war. My strongest feelings were engaged in this struggle, which, I felt from the beginning, was destined to be a turning point, for good or evil, of the course of human affairs for an indefinite duration. Having been a deeply interested observer of the Slavery quarrel in America, during the many years that preceded the open breach, I knew that it was in all its stages an aggressive enterprise of the slave-owners to extend the territory of slavery; under the combined influences of pecuniary interest, domineering temper, and the fanaticism of a class for its class privileges, influences so fully and powerfully depicted in the admirable work of my friend Professor Cairnes, " The Slave Power." Their success, if they succeeded, would be a victory of the powers of evil which would give courage to the enemies of progress and damp the spirits of its friends all over the civilized world, while it would create a formidable military power, grounded on the worst and most anti-social form of the tyranny of men over men, and, by destroying for a long time the prestige of the great democratic republic, would give to all the privileged classes of Europe a false confidence, probably only to be extinguished in blood. On the other hand, if the spirit of the North was sufficiently roused to carry the war to a successful termination, and if that termination did not come too soon and too easily, I foresaw, from the laws of human nature, and the experience of revolutions, that when it did come it would in all probability be thorough: that the bulk of the Northern population, whose conscience had as yet been awakened only to the point of resisting the further extension of slavery, but whose fidelity to the Constitution of the United States made them disapprove of any attempt by the Federal Government to interfere with slavery in the States where it already existed, would acquire feelings of another kind when the Constitution had been shaken off by armed rebellion, would determine to have done for ever with the accursed thing, and would join their banner with that of the noble body of Abolitionists, of whom Garrison was the courageous and single-minded apostle, Wendell Phillips the eloquent orator, and John Brown the voluntary martyr.[1] Then, too, the whole mind of the United States would be let loose from its bonds, no longer corrupted by the supposed necessity of apologizing to foreigners for the most flagrant of all possible violations of the free principles of their Constitution; while the tendency of a fixed state of society to stereotype a set of national opinions would be at least temporarily checked, and the national mind would become more open to the recognition of whatever was bad in either the institutions or the customs of the people. These hopes, so far as related to Slavery, have been completely, and in other respects are in course of being progressively realized. Foreseeing from the first this double set of consequences from the success or failure of the rebellion, it may be imagined with what feelings I contemplated the rush of nearly the whole upper and middle classes of my own country, even those who passed for Liberals, into a furious pro-Southern partisanship: the working classes, and some of the literary and scientific men, being almost the sole exceptions to the general frenzy. I never before felt so keenly how little permanent improvement had reached the minds of our influential classes, and of what small value were the liberal opinions they had got into the habit of professing. None of the Continental Liberals committed the same frightful mistake. But the generation which had extorted negro emancipation from

---

[1] The saying of this true hero, after his capture, that he was worth more for hanging than for any other purpose, reminds one, by its combination of wit, wisdom, and self-devotion, of Sir Thomas More.

our West India planters had passed away; another had succeeded which had not learnt by many years of discussion and exposure to feel strongly the enormities of slavery; and the inattention habitual with Englishmen to whatever is going on in the world outside their own island, made them profoundly ignorant of all the antecedents of the struggle, insomuch that it was not generally believed in England, for the first year or two of the war, that the quarrel was one of slavery. There were men of high principle and unquestionable liberality of opinion, who thought it a dispute about tariffs, or assimilated it to the cases in which they were accustomed to sympathize, of a people struggling for independence.

It was my obvious duty to be one of the small minority who protested against this perverted state of public opinion. I was not the first to protest. It ought to be remembered to the honour of Mr. Hughes and of Mr. Ludlow, that they, by writings published at the very beginning of the struggle, began the protestation. Mr. Bright followed in one of the most powerful of his speeches, followed by others not less striking. I was on the point of adding my words to theirs, when there occurred, towards the end of 1861, the seizure of the Southern envoys on board a British vessel, by an officer of the United States. Even English forgetfulness has not yet had time to lose all remembrance of the explosion of feeling in England which then burst forth, the expectation, prevailing for some weeks, of war with the United States, and the warlike preparations actually commenced on this side. While this state of things lasted, there was no chance of a hearing for anything favourable to the American cause; and, moreover, I agreed with those who thought the act unjustifiable, and such as to require that England should demand its disavowal. When the disavowal came, and the alarm of war was over, I wrote, in January, 1862, the paper, in Fraser's Magazine, entitled " The Contest in America." And I shall always feel grateful to my daughter that her urgency prevailed on me to write it when I did, for we were then on the point of setting out for a journey of some months in Greece and Turkey, and but for her, I should have deferred writing till our return. Written and published when it was, this paper helped to encourage those Liberals who had felt overborne by the tide of illiberal opinion, and to form in favour of the good cause a nucleus of opinion which increased gradually, and, after the success of the North began to seem probable, rapidly. When we returned from our journey I wrote a second article, a review of Professor Cairnes' book, published in the Westminster Review. England is paying the penalty, in many uncomfortable ways, of the durable resentment which her ruling classes stirred up in the United States by their ostentatious wishes for the ruin of America as a nation: they have reason to be thankful that a few, if only a few, known writers and speakers, standing firmly by the Americans in the time of their greatest difficulty, effected a partial diversion of these bitter feelings, and made Great Britain not altogether odious to the Americans.

This duty having been performed, my principal occupation for the next two years was on subjects not political. The publication of Mr. Austin's Lectures on Jurisprudence after his decease, gave me an opportunity of paying a deserved tribute to his memory, and at the same time expressing some thoughts on a subject on which, in my old days of Benthamism, I had bestowed much study. But the chief product of those years was the Examination of Sir William Hamilton's Philosophy. His Lectures, published in 1860 and 1861, I had read towards the end of the latter year, with a half-formed intention of giving an account of them in a Review, but I soon found that this would be idle, and that justice could not be done to the subject in less than a volume. I had then to consider whether it would be advisable that I myself should attempt such a performance. On consideration, there seemed to be strong reasons for doing so. I was greatly disappointed with the Lectures. I read them, certainly, with no prejudice against Sir W. Hamilton. I had up to that time deferred the study of his Notes to Reid on account of their unfinished state, but I had not neglected his " Discussions in Philosophy; " and though I knew that his general mode of treating the facts of mental philosophy differed from that of which I most approved, yet his vigorous polemic against the later Transcendentalists, and his strenuous assertion of some important principles, especially the Relativity of human knowledge, gave me many points of sympathy with his opinions, and made me think that genuine psychology had considerably more to gain than to lose by his authority and reputation. His Lectures and the Dissertations on Reid dispelled this illusion: and even the Discussions, read by the light which these throw on them, lost much of their value. I found that the points of apparent agreement between his opinions and mine were more verbal than real; that the important philosophical principles which I had thought he recognised, were so explained away by him as to mean little or nothing, or were continually lost sight of, and doctrines entirely inconsistent with them were taught in nearly every part of his philosophical writings. My estimation of him was therefore so far altered, that instead of regarding him as occupying a kind of intermediate position between the two rival philosophies, holding some of the principles of both, and supplying to both powerful weapons of attack and defence, I now looked upon him as one of the pillars, and in this country from his high philosophical reputation the chief pillar, of that one of the two which seemed to me to be erroneous.

Now, the difference between these two schools of philosophy, that of Intuition, and that of Experience and Association, is not a mere matter of abstract speculation; it is full of practical consequences, and lies at the foundation of all the greatest differences of practical opinion in an age of progress. The practical reformer has continually to demand that changes be made in things which are supported by powerful and widely-spread feelings, or to question the apparent necessity and indefeasibleness of established facts; and it is often an indispensable part of his argument to show, how those powerful feelings had their origin, and how those facts came to seem necessary and indefeasible. There is therefore a natural hostility between him and a philosophy which discourages the explanation of feelings and moral facts by circumstances and association, and prefers to treat them as ultimate elements of human nature; a philosophy which is addicted to holding up favourite doctrines as intuitive truths, and deems intuition to be the voice of Nature and of God, speaking with an authority higher than that of our reason. In particular, I have long felt that the prevailing tendency to regard all the marked distinctions of human character as innate, and in the main indelible, and to ignore the irresistible proofs that by far the greater part of those differences, whether between individuals, races, or sexes, are such as not only might but naturally would be produced by differences in circumstances, is one of the chief hindrances to the rational treatment of great social questions, and one of the greatest stumbling blocks to human improvement. This tendency has its source in the intuitional metaphysics which characterized the reaction of the nineteenth century against the eighteenth, and it is a tendency so agreeable to human indolence, as well as to conservative interests generally, that unless attacked at the very root, it is sure to be carried to even a greater length than is really justified by the more moderate forms of the intuitional philosophy. That philosophy, not always in its moderate forms, had ruled the thought of Europe for the greater part of a century. My father's Analysis of the Mind, my own Logic, and Professor Bain's great treatise, had attempted to re-introduce a better mode of philosophizing, latterly with quite as much success as could be expected; but I had for some time felt that the mere contrast of the two philosophies was not enough, that there ought to be a hand-to-hand fight between them, that controversial as well as expository writings were needed, and that the time was come when such controversy would be useful. Considering then the writings and fame of Sir W. Hamilton as the great fortress of the intuitional philosophy in this country, a fortress the more formidable from the imposing character, and the in many respects great personal merits and mental endowments, of the man, I thought it might be a real service to philosophy to attempt a thorough examination of all his most important doctrines, and an estimate of his general claims to eminence as a philosopher, and I was confirmed in this resolution by observing that in the writings of at least one, and him one of the ablest, of Sir W. Hamilton's followers, his peculiar doctrines were made the justification of a view of religion which I hold to be profoundly immoral — that it is our duty to bow down in worship before a Being whose moral attributes are affirmed to be unknowable by us, and to be perhaps extremely different from those which, when we are speaking of our fellow creatures, we call by the same names.

As I advanced in my task, the damage to Sir W. Hamilton's reputation became greater than I at first expected, through the almost incredible multitude of inconsistencies which showed themselves on comparing different passages with one another. It was my business, however, to show things exactly as they were, and I did not flinch from it. I endeavoured always to treat the philosopher whom I criticized with the most scrupulous fairness; and I knew that he had abundance of disciples and admirers to correct me if I ever unintentionally did him injustice. Many of them accordingly have answered me, more or less elaborately; and they have pointed out oversights and misunderstandings, though few in number, and mostly very unimportant in substance. Such of those as had (to my knowledge) been pointed out before the publication of the latest edition (at present the third) have been corrected there, and the remainder of the criticisms have been, as far as seemed necessary, replied to. On the whole, the book has done its work: it has shown the weak side of Sir W. Hamilton, and has reduced his too great philosophical reputation within more moderate bounds; and by some of its discussions, as well as by two expository chapters, on the notions of Matter and of Mind, it has perhaps thrown additional light on some of the disputed questions in the domain of psychology and metaphysics.

After the completion of the book on Hamilton, I applied myself to a task which a variety of reasons seemed to render specially incumbent upon me; that of giving an account, and forming an estimate, of the doctrines of Auguste Comte. I had contributed more than any one else to make his speculations known in England. In consequence chiefly of what I had said of him in my Logic, he had readers and admirers among thoughtful men on this side of the Channel at a time when his name had not yet in France emerged from obscurity. So unknown and unappreciated was he at the time when my Logic was written and published, that to criticize his weak points might well appear superfluous, while it was a duty to give as much publicity as one could to the important contributions he had made to philosophic thought. At the time, however, at which I have now arrived, this state of affairs had entirely changed. His name, at least, was known almost universally, and the general character of his doctrines very widely. He had taken his place in the estimation both of friends and opponents, as one of the conspicuous figures in the thought of the age. The better parts of his speculations had made great progress in working their way into those minds, which, by their previous culture and tendencies, were fitted to receive them: under cover of those

better parts those of a worse character, greatly developed
and added to in his later writings, had also made some
way, having obtained active and enthusiastic adherents,
some of them of no inconsiderable personal merit, in
England, France, and other countries. These causes not
only made it desirable that some one should undertake the
task of sifting what is good from what is bad in M.
Comte's speculations, but seemed to impose on myself in
particular a special obligation to make the attempt. This
I accordingly did in two Essays, published in successive
numbers of the Westminster Review, and reprinted in a
small volume under the title " Auguste Comte and
Positivism."

The writings which I have now mentioned, together
with a small number of papers in periodicals which I have
not deemed worth preserving, were the whole of the
products of my activity as a writer during the years from
1859 to 1865. In the early part of the last-mentioned
year, in compliance with a wish frequently expressed to
me by working men, I published cheap People's Editions
of those of my writings which seemed the most likely to
find readers among the working classes; viz, Principles of
Political Economy, Liberty, and Representative Government. This was a considerable sacrifice of my pecuniary
interest, especially as I resigned all idea of deriving profit
from the cheap editions, and after ascertaining from my
publishers the lowest price which they thought would re-
munerate them on the usual terms of an equal division of
profits, I gave up my half share to enable the price to be
fixed still lower. To the credit of Messrs. Longman they
fixed, unasked, a certain number of years after which the
copyright and stereotype plates were to revert to me, and
a certain number of copies after the sale of which I should
receive half of any further profit. This number of copies
(which in the case of the Political Economy was 10,000)
has for some time been exceeded, and the People's Editions

have begun to yield me a small but unexpected pecuniary return, though very far from an equivalent for the diminution of profit from the Library Editions.

In this summary of my outward life I have now arrived at the period at which my tranquil and retired existence as a writer of books was to be exchanged for the less congenial occupation of a member of the House of Commons. The proposal made to me, early in 1865, by some electors of Westminster, did not present the idea to me for the first time. It was not even the first offer I had received, for, more than ten years previous, in consequence of my opinions on the Irish Land question, Mr. Lucas and Mr. Duffy, in the name of the popular party in Ireland, offered to bring me into Parliament for an Irish County, which they could easily have done: but the incompatibility of a seat in Parliament with the office I then held in the India House, precluded even consideration of the proposal. After I had quitted the India House, several of my friends would gladly have seen me a member of Parliament; but there seemed no probability that the idea would ever take any practical shape. I was convinced that no numerous or influential portion of any electoral body, really wished to be represented by a person of my opinions; and that one who possessed no local connexion or popularity, and who did not choose to stand as the mere organ of a party, had small chance of being elected anywhere unless through the expenditure of money. Now it was, and is, my fixed conviction, that a candidate ought not to incur one farthing of expense for undertaking a public duty. Such of the lawful expenses of an election as have no special reference to any particular candidate, ought to be borne as a public charge, either by the State or by the locality. What has to be done by the supporters of each candidate in order to bring his claims properly before the constituency, should be done by unpaid agency, or by voluntary subscription. If members of the electoral body, or others, are willing

to subscribe money of their own for the purpose of bringing, by lawful means, into Parliament some one who they
think would be useful there, no one is entitled to object:
but that the expense, or any part of it, should fall on the
candidate, is fundamentally wrong; because it amounts in
reality to buying his seat. Even on the most favourable
supposition as to the mode in which the money is expended,
there is a legitimate suspicion that any one who gives money
for leave to undertake a public trust, has other than public
ends to promote by it; and (a consideration of the greatest
importance) the cost of elections, when borne by the candidates, deprives the nation of the services, as members of
Parliament, of all who cannot or will not afford to incur
a heavy expense. I do not say that, so long as there is
scarcely a chance for an independent candidate to come into
Parliament without complying with this vicious practice,
it must always be morally wrong in him to spend money,
provided that no part of it is either directly or indirectly
employed in corruption. But, to justify it, he ought to be
very certain that he can be of more use to his country as
a member of Parliament than in any other mode which is
open to him; and this assurance, in my own case, I did not
feel. It was by no means clear to me that I could do more
to advance the public objects which had a claim on my
exertions, from the benches of the House of Commons,
than from the simple position of a writer. I felt, therefore, that I ought not to seek election to Parliament, much
less to expend any money in procuring it.

But the conditions of the question were considerably
altered when a body of electors sought me out, and spontaneously offered to bring me forward as their candidate.
If it should appear, on explanation, that they persisted in
this wish, knowing my opinions, and accepting the only
conditions on which I could conscientiously serve, it was
questionable whether this was not one of those calls upon
a member of the community by his fellow-citizens, which

he was scarcely justified in rejecting. I therefore put their disposition to the proof by one of the frankest explanations ever tendered, I should think, to an electoral body by a candidate. I wrote, in reply to the offer, a letter for publication, saying that I had no personal wish to be a member of parliament, that I thought a candidate ought neither to canvass nor to incur any expense, and that I could not consent to do either. I said further, that if elected, I could not undertake to give any of my time and labour to their local interests. With respect to general politics, I told them without reserve, what I thought on a number of important subjects on which they had asked my opinion; and one of these being the suffrage, I made known to them, among other things, my conviction (as I was bound to do, since I intended, if elected, to act on it), that women were entitled to representation in Parliament on the same terms with men. It was the first time, doubtless, that such a doctrine had ever been mentioned to English electors; and the fact that I was elected after proposing it, gave the start to the movement which has since become so vigorous, in favour of women's suffrage. Nothing, at the time, appeared more unlikely than that a candidate (if candidate I could be called) whose professions and conduct set so completely at defiance all ordinary notions of electioneering, should nevertheless be elected. A well-known literary man, who was also a man of society, was heard to say that the Almighty himself would have no chance of being elected on such a programme. I strictly adhered to it, neither spending money nor canvassing, nor did I take any personal part in the election, until about a week preceding the day of nomination, when I attended a few public meetings to state my principles and give to any questions which the electors might exercise their just right of putting to me for their own guidance, answers as plain and unreserved as my Address. On one subject only, my religious opinions, I announced from the beginning that I would answer no questions; a determination which appeared to be completely approved by those who attended the meetings. My frankness on all other subjects on which I was interrogated, evidently did me far more good than my answers, whatever they might be, did harm. Among the proofs I received of this, one is too remarkable not to be recorded. In the pamphlet, " Thoughts on Parliamentary Reform," I had said, rather bluntly, that the working classes, though differing from those of some other countries, in being ashamed of lying, are yet generally liars. This passage some opponent got printed in a placard, which was handed to me at a meeting, chiefly composed of the working classes, and I was asked whether I had written and published it. I at once answered " I did." Scarcely were these two words out of my mouth, when vehement applause resounded through the whole meeting. It was evident that the working people were so accustomed to expect equivocation and evasion from those who sought their suffrages, that when they found, instead of that, a direct avowal of what was likely to be disagreeable to them, instead of being offended, they concluded at once that this was a person whom they could trust. A more striking instance never came under my notice of what, I believe, is the experience of those who best know the working classes, that the most essential of all recommendations to their favour is that of complete straightforwardness; its presence outweighs in their minds very strong objections, while no amount of other qualities will make amends for its apparent absence. The first working man who spoke after the incident I have mentioned (it was Mr. Odger) said, that the working classes had no desire not to be told of their faults; they wanted friends, not flatterers, and felt under obligation to any one who told them anything in themselves which he sincerely believed to require amendment. And to this the meeting heartily responded.

Had I been defeated in the election, I should still have

had no reason to regret the contact it had brought me into with large bodies of my countrymen; which not only gave me much new experience, but enabled me to scatter my political opinions rather widely, and, by making me known in many quarters where I had never before been heard of, increased the number of my readers, and the presumable influence of my writings. These latter effects were of course produced in a still greater degree, when, as much to my surprise as to that of any one, I was returned to Parliament by a majority of some hundreds over my Conservative competitor.

I was a member of the House during the three sessions of the Parliament which passed the Reform Bill; during which time Parliament was necessarily my main occupation, except during the recess. I was a tolerably frequent speaker, sometimes of prepared speeches, sometimes extemporaneously. But my choice of occasions was not such as I should have made if my leading object had been parliamentary influence. When I had gained the ear of the House, which I did by a successful speech on Mr. Gladstone's Reform Bill, the idea I proceeded on was that when anything was likely to be as well done, or sufficiently well done, by other people, there was no necessity for me to meddle with it. As I, therefore, in general reserved myself for work which no others were likely to do, a great proportion of my appearances were on points on which the bulk of the Liberal party, even the advanced portion of it, either were of a different opinion from mine, or were comparatively indifferent. Several of my speeches, especially one against the motion for the abolition of capital punishment, and another in favour of resuming the right of seizing enemies' goods in neutral vessels, were opposed to what then was, and probably still is, regarded as the advanced liberal opinion. My advocacy of women's suffrage and of Personal Representation, were at the time looked upon by many as whims of my own; but the great progress since made by those opinions, and especially the zealous response made from almost all parts of the kingdom to the demand for women's suffrage, fully justified the timeliness of those movements, and have made what was undertaken as a moral and social duty, a personal success. Another duty which was particularly incumbent on me as one of the Metropolitan Members, was the attempt to obtain a Municipal Government for the Metropolis: but on that subject the indifference of the House of Commons was such that I found hardly any help or support within its walls. On this subject, however, I was the organ of an active and intelligent body of persons outside, with whom, and not with me, the scheme originated, and who carried on all the agitation on the subject and drew up the Bills. My part was to bring in Bills already prepared, and to sustain the discussion of them during the short time they were allowed to remain before the House; after having taken an active part in the work of a Committee presided over by Mr. Ayrton, which sat through the greater part of the Session of 1866, to take evidence on the subject. The very different position in which the question now stands (1870) may justly be attributed to the preparation which went on during those years, and which produced but little visible effect at the time; but all questions on which there are strong private interests on one side, and only the public good on the other, have a similar period of incubation to go through.

The same idea, that the use of my being in Parliament was to do work which others were not able or not willing to do, made me think it my duty to come to the front in defence of advanced Liberalism on occasions when the obloquy to be encountered was such as most of the advanced Liberals in the House, preferred not to incur. My first vote in the House was in support of an amendment in favour of Ireland, moved by an Irish member, and for which only five English and Scotch votes were given,

including my own: the other four were Mr. Bright, Mr.
McLaren, Mr. T. B. Potter, and Mr. Hadfield. And
the second speech I delivered[1] was on the bill to prolong
the suspension of the Habeas Corpus in Ireland. In de-
nouncing, on this occasion, the English mode of governing Ireland, I did no more than the general opinion of
England now admits to have been just; but the anger
against Fenianism was then in all its freshness; any attack
on what Fenians attacked was looked upon as an apology
for them; and I was so unfavourably received by the
House, that more than one of my friends advised me (and
my own judgment agreed with the advice) to wait, before
speaking again, for the favourable opportunity that would be
given by the first great debate on the Reform Bill. During
this silence, many flattered themselves that I had turned
out a failure, and that they should not be troubled with
me any more. Perhaps their uncomplimentary comments
may, by the force of reaction, have helped to make my
speech on the Reform Bill the success it was. My position
in the House was further improved by a speech in which
I insisted on the duty of paying off the National Debt
before our coal supplies are exhausted, and by an ironical
reply to some of the Tory leaders who had quoted against
me certain passages of my writings, and called me to account
for others, especially for one in my "Considerations on
Representative Government," which said that the Conservative party was, by the law of its composition, the
stupidest party. They gained nothing by drawing attention to the passage, which up to that time had not excited
any notice, but the *sobriquet* of "the stupid party" stuck

---

[1] The first was in answer to Mr. Lowe's reply to Mr. Bright on the
Cattle Plague Bill, and was thought at the time to have helped to get
rid of a provision in the Government measure which would have given
to landholders a second indemnity, after they had already been once
indemnified for the loss of some of their cattle by the increased selling
price of the remainder.

to them for a considerable time afterwards. Having now no longer any apprehension of not being listened to, I confined myself, as I have since thought too much, to occasions on which my services seemed specially needed, and abstained more than enough from speaking on the great party questions. With the exception of Irish questions, and those which concerned the working classes, a single speech on Mr. Disraeli's Reform Bill was nearly all that I contributed to the great decisive debates of the last two of my three sessions.

I have, however, much satisfaction in looking back to the part I took on the two classes of subjects just mentioned. With regard to the working classes, the chief topic of my speech on Mr. Gladstone's Reform Bill was the assertion of their claims to the suffrage. A little later, after the resignation of Lord Russell's ministry and the succession of a Tory Government, came the attempt of the working classes to hold a meeting in Hyde Park, their exclusion by the police, and the breaking down of the park railing by the crowd. Though Mr. Beales and the leaders of the working men had retired under protest before this took place, a scuffle ensued in which many innocent persons were maltreated by the police, and the exasperation of the working men was extreme. They showed a determination to make another attempt at a meeting in the Park, to which many of them would probably have come armed; the Government made military preparations to resist the attempt, and something very serious seemed impending. At this crisis I really believe that I was the means of preventing much mischief. I had in my place in Parliament taken the side of the working men, and strongly censured the conduct of the Government. I was invited, with several other Radical members, to a conference with the leading members of the Council of the Reform League; and the task fell chiefly upon myself, of persuading them to give up the Hyde Park project, and hold their meeting elsewhere. It was not Mr. Beales and Colonel Dickson who needed persuading; on the contrary, it was evident that these gentlemen had already exerted their influence in the same direction, thus far without success. It was the working men who held out, and so bent were they on their original scheme, that I was obliged to have recourse to *les grands moyens*. I told them that a proceeding which would certainly produce a collision with the military, could only be justifiable on two conditions: if the position of affairs had become such that a revolution was desirable, and if they thought themselves able to accomplish one. To this argument, after considerable discussion, they at last yielded: and I was able to inform Mr. Walpole that their intention was given up. I shall never forget the depth of his relief or the warmth of his expressions of gratitude. After the working men had conceded so much to me, I felt bound to comply with their request that I would attend and speak at their meeting at the Agricultural Hall; the only meeting called by the Reform League which I ever attended. I had always declined being a member of the League, on the avowed ground that I did not agree in its programme of manhood suffrage and the ballot: from the ballot I dissented entirely; and I could not consent to hoist the flag of manhood suffrage, even on the assurance that the exclusion of women was not intended to be implied; since if one goes beyond what can be immediately carried, and professes to take one's stand on a principle, one should go the whole length of the principle. I have entered thus particularly into this matter because my conduct on this occasion gave great displeasure to the Tory and Tory-Liberal press, who have charged me ever since with having shown myself, in the trials of public life, intemperate and passionate. I do not know what they expected from me; but they had reason to be thankful to me if they knew from what I had, in all probability, preserved them. And I do not believe it could have been done, at that particular juncture, by any one else. No other person, I believe, had at that moment the necessary influence for restraining the working classes, except Mr. Gladstone and Mr. Bright, neither of whom was available: Mr. Gladstone, for obvious reasons; Mr. Bright because he was out of town.

When, some time later, the Tory Government brought in a bill to prevent public meetings in the Parks, I not only spoke strongly in opposition to it, but formed one of a number of advanced Liberals, who, aided by the very late period of the Session, succeeded in defeating the Bill by what is called talking it out. It has not since been renewed.

On Irish affairs also I felt bound to take a decided part. I was one of the foremost in the deputation of Members of Parliament who prevailed on Lord Derby to spare the life of the condemned Fenian insurgent, General Burke. The Church question was so vigorously handled by the leaders of the party, in the session of 1868, as to require no more from me than an emphatic adhesion: but the land question was by no means in so advanced a position; the superstitions of landlordism had up to that time been little challenged, especially in Parliament, and the backward state of the question, so far as concerned the Parliamentary mind, was evidenced by the extremely mild measure brought in by Lord Russell's Government in 1866, which nevertheless could not be carried. On that bill I delivered one of my most careful speeches, in which I attempted to lay down some of the principles of the subject, in a manner calculated less to stimulate frends, than to conciliate and convince opponents. The engrossing subject of Parliamentary Reform prevented either this bill, or one of a similar character brought in by Lord Derby's Government, from being carried through. They never got beyond the second reading. Meanwhile the signs of Irish disaffection had become much more decided; the demand for complete separation between the two countries had assumed a menacing aspect, and there

were few who did not feel that if there was still any chance
of reconciling Ireland to the British connexion, it could
only be by the adoption of much more thorough reforms
in the territorial and social relations of the country, than
had yet been contemplated. The time seemed to me to
have come when it would be useful to speak out my whole
mind; and the result was my pamphlet " England and
Ireland," which was written in the winter of 1867, and
published shortly before the commencement of the session
of 1868. The leading features of the pamphlet were, on
the one hand, an argument to show the undesirableness,
for Ireland as well as England, of separation between the
countries, and on the other, a proposal for settling the
land question by giving to the existing tenants a permanent tenure, at a fixed rent, to be assessed after due inquiry
by the State.

The pamphlet was not popular, except in Ireland, as I
did not expect it to be. But, if no measure short of that
which I proposed would do full justice to Ireland, or
afford a prospect of conciliating the mass of the Irish
people, the duty of proposing it was imperative; while if,
on the other hand, there was any intermediate course
which had a claim to a trial, I well knew that to propose
something which would be called extreme, was the true
way not to impede but to facilitate a more moderate experiment. It is most improbable that a measure conceding so
much to the tenantry as Mr. Gladstone's Irish Land Bill,
would have been proposed by a Government, or could have
been carried through Parliament, unless the British public
had been led to perceive that a case might be made, and
perhaps a party formed, for a measure considerably
stronger. It is the character of the British people, or at
least of the higher and middle classes who pass muster for
the British people, that to induce them to approve of any
change, it is necessary that they should look upon it as a
middle course: they think every proposal extreme and

violent unless they hear of some other proposal going still farther, upon which their antipathy to extreme views may discharge itself. So it proved in the present instance; my proposal was condemned, but any scheme of Irish Land reform, short of mine, came to be thought moderate by comparison. I may observe that the attacks made on my plan usually gave a very incorrect idea of its nature. It was usually discussed as a proposal that the State should buy up the land and become the universal landlord; though in fact it only offered to each individual landlord this as an alternative, if he liked better to sell his estate than to retain it on the new conditions; and I fully anticipated that most landlords would continue to prefer the position of landowners to that of Government annuitants, and would retain their existing relation to their tenants, often on more indulgent terms than the full rents on which the compensation to be given them by Government would have been based. This and many other explanations I gave in a speech on Ireland, in the debate on Mr. Maguire's Resolution, early in the session of 1868. A corrected report of this speech, together with my speech on Mr. Fortescue's Bill, has been published (not by me, but with my permission) in Ireland.

Another public duty, of a most serious kind, it was my lot to have to perform, both in and out of Parliament, during these years. A disturbance in Jamaica, provoked in the first instance by injustice, and exaggerated by rage and panic into a premeditated rebellion, had been the motive or excuse for taking hundreds of innocent lives by military violence, or by sentence of what were called courts-martial, continuing for weeks after the brief disturbance had been put down; with many added atrocities of destruction of property, flogging women as well as men, and a general display of the brutal recklessness which usually prevails when fire and sword are let loose. The perpetrators of those deeds were defended and applauded

in England by the same kind of people who had so long
upheld negro slavery: and it seemed at first as if the
British nation was about to incur the disgrace of letting
pass without even a protest, excesses of authority as revolt-
ing as any of those for which, when perpetrated by the
instruments of other governments, Englishmen can hardly
find terms sufficient to express their abhorrence. After a
short time, however, an indignant feeling was roused: a
voluntary Association formed itself under the name of
the Jamaica Committee, to take such deliberation and
action as the case might admit of, and adhesions poured in
from all parts of the country. I was abroad at the time,
but I sent in my name to the Committee as soon as I heard
of it, and took an active part in the proceedings from the
time of my return. There was much more at stake than
only justice to the Negroes, imperative as was that consideration. The question was, whether the British depend-
encies, and eventually, perhaps, Great Britain itself, were
to be under the government of law, or of military licence;
whether the lives and persons of British subjects are at
the mercy of any two or three officers however raw and
inexperienced or reckless and brutal, whom a panic-stricken
Governor, or other functionary, may assume the right to
constitute into a so-called Court-martial. This question
could only be decided by an appeal to the tribunals; and
such an appeal the Committee determined to make. Their
determination led to a change in the Chairmanship of the
Committee, as the Chairman, Mr. Charles Buxton, thought
it not unjust indeed, but inexpedient, to prosecute Governor
Eyre and his principal subordinates in a criminal court: but
a numerously attended general meeting of the Association
having decided this point against him, Mr. Buxton withdrew from the Committee, though continuing to work in
the cause, and I was, quite unexpectedly on my own part,
proposed and elected Chairman. It became, in consequence, my duty to represent the Committee in the House,

sometimes by putting questions to the Government, sometimes as the recipient of questions, more or less provocative, addressed by individual members to myself; but especially as speaker in the important debate originated in the session of 1866, by Mr. Buxton: and the speech I then delivered is that which I should probably select as the best of my speeches in Parliament.[1] For more than two years we carried on the combat, trying every avenue legally open to us, to the courts of criminal justice. A bench of magistrates in one of the most Tory counties in England dismissed our case: we were more successful before the magistrates at Bow Street; which gave an opportunity to the Lord Chief Justice of the Queen's Bench, Sir Alexander Cockburn, for delivering his celebrated charge, which settled the law of the question in favour of liberty, as far as it is in the power of a judge's charge to settle it. There, however, our success ended, for the Old Bailey Grand Jury by throwing out our bill prevented the case from coming to trial. It was clear that to bring English functionaries to the bar of a criminal court for abuses of power committed against negroes and mulattoes was not a popular proceeding with the English middle classes. We had, however, redeemed, so far as lay in us, the character of our country, by showing that there was at any rate a body of persons determined to use all the means which the law afforded to obtain justice for the injured. We had elicited from the highest criminal judge in the nation an authoritative declaration that the law was what we maintained it to be; and we had given an emphatic warning to those who might be tempted to similar guilt hereafter, that, though they might escape the actual sentence of a criminal

---

[1] Among the most active members of the Committee were Mr. P. A. Taylor, M.P., always faithful and energetic in every assertion of the principles of liberty; Mr. Goldwin Smith, Mr. Frederic Harrison, Mr. Slack, Mr. Chamerovzow, Mr. Shaen, and Mr. Chesson, the Honorary Secretary of the Association.

tribunal, they were not safe against being put to some
trouble and expense in order to avoid it. Colonial gov-
ernors and other persons in authority, will have a considerable motive to stop short of such extremities in future.

As a matter of curiosity I kept some specimens of the
abusive letters, almost all of them anonymous, which I
received while these proceedings were going on. They
are evidence of the sympathy felt with the brutalities in
Jamaica by the brutal part of the population at home.
They graduated from coarse jokes, verbal and pictorial, up
to threats of[1] assassination.

Among other matters of importance in which I took an
active part, but which excited little interest in the public,
two deserve particular mention. I joined with several
other independent Liberals in defeating an Extradition
Bill introduced at the very end of the session of 1866, and
by which, though surrender avowedly for political offences
was not authorized, political refugees, if charged by a
foreign government with acts which are necessarily incident
to all attempts at insurrection, would have been surrendered
to be dealt with by the criminal courts of the government
against which they had rebelled: thus making the British
Government an accomplice in the vengeance of foreign
despotisms. The defeat of this proposal led to the
appointment of a Select Committee (in which I was included), to examine and report on the whole subject of
Extradition Treaties; and the result was, that in the Extradition Act which passed through Parliament after I had
ceased to be a member, opportunity is given to any one

---

[1] At one time I reckoned that threats of assassination were received
at least once a week; and I remarked that threatening letters were
always especially numerous by Tuesday morning's post. I inferred that
they were meditated during the Sunday's leisure and posted on the
Mondays. It might be worth while to collect evidence as to the
proportions of crime committed on the different days of the week.
It may be observed however that in England Sunday is generally used
for all kinds of letter-writing, innocent as well as guilty. Helen Taylor.

whose extradition is demanded, of being heard before an English Court of justice to prove that the offence with which he is charged, is really political. The cause of European freedom has thus been saved from a serious misfortune, and our own country from a great iniquity. The other subject to be mentioned is the fight kept up by a body of advanced Liberals in the session of 1868, on the Bribery Bill of Mr. Disraeli's Government, in which I took a very active part. I had taken counsel with several of those who had applied their minds most carefully to the details of the subject — Mr. W. D. Christie, Serjeant Pulling, Mr. Chadwick — as well as bestowed much thought of my own, for the purpose of framing such amendments and additional clauses as might make the Bill really effective against the numerous modes of corruption, direct and indirect, which might otherwise, as there was much reason to fear, be increased instead of diminished by the Reform Act. We also aimed at engrafting on the Bill, measures for diminishing the mischievous burthen of what are called the legitimate expenses of elections. Among our many amendments, was that of Mr. Fawcett for making the returning officer's expenses a charge on the rates, instead of on the candidates; another was the prohibition of paid canvassers, and the limitation of paid agents to one for each candidate; a third was the extension of the precautions and penalties against bribery, to municipal elections, which are well known to be not only a preparatory school for bribery at parliamentary elections, but an habitual cover for it. The Conservative Government, however, when once they had carried the leading provision of their Bill (for which I voted and spoke), the transfer of the jurisdiction in elections from the House of Commons to the Judges, made a determined resistance to all other improvements; and after one of our most important proposals, that of Mr. Fawcett, had actually obtained a majority, they summoned the strength of their party and threw out the clause in a subsequent stage. The Liberal party in the House was greatly dishonoured by the conduct of many of its members in giving no help whatever to this attempt to secure the necessary conditions of an honest representation of the people. With their large majority in the House they could have carried all the amendments, or better ones if they had better to propose. But it was late in the Session; members were eager to set about their preparations for the impending General Election: and while some (such as Sir Robert Anstruther) honourably remained at their post, though rival candidates were already canvassing their constituency, a much greater number placed their electioneering interests before their public duty. Many Liberals also looked with indifference on legislation against bribery, thinking that it merely diverted public interest from the Ballot, which they considered, very mistakenly as I expect it will turn out, to be a sufficient, and the only, remedy. From these causes our fight, though kept up with great vigour for several nights, was wholly unsuccessful, and the practices which we sought to render more difficult, prevailed more widely than ever in the first General Election held under the new electoral law.

In the general debates on Mr. Disraeli's Reform Bill, my participation was limited to the one speech already mentioned; but I made the Bill an occasion for bringing the two greatest improvements which remain to be made in representative government, formally before the House and the nation. One of them was Personal, or, as it is called with equal propriety, Proportional Representation. I brought this under the consideration of the House, by an expository and argumentative speech on Mr. Hare's plan; and subsequently I was active in support of the very imperfect substitute for that plan, which, in a small number of constituencies, Parliament was induced to adopt. This poor makeshift had scarcely any recommendation, except that it was a partial recognition of the evil which it did so little to remedy. As such, however, it was attacked by the same fallacies, and required to be defended on the same principles, as a really good measure; and its adoption in a few parliamentary elections, as well as the subsequent introduction of what is called the Cumulative Vote in the elections for the London School Board, have had the good effect of converting the equal claim of all electors to a proportional share in the representation, from a subject of merely speculative discussion, into a question of practical politics, much sooner than would otherwise have been the case.

This assertion of my opinions on Personal Representation cannot be credited with any considerable or visible amount of practical result. It was otherwise with the other motion which I made in the form of an amendment to the Reform Bill, and which was by far the most important, perhaps the only really important, public service I performed in the capacity of a Member of Parliament: a motion to strike out the words which were understood to limit the electoral franchise to males, and thereby admitting to the suffrage all women who, as householders or otherwise, possessed the qualification required of male electors. For women not to make their claim to the suffrage, at the time when the elective franchise was being largely extended, would have been to abjure the claim altogether; and a movement on the subject was begun in 1866, when I presented a petition for the suffrage, signed by a considerable number of distinguished women. But it was as yet uncertain whether the proposal would obtain more than a few stray votes in the House: and when, after a debate in which the speakers on the contrary side were conspicuous by their feebleness, the votes recorded in favour of the motion amounted to 73 — made up by pairs and tellers to above 80 — the surprise was general, and the encouragement great: the greater, too, because one of those who voted for the motion was Mr. Bright, a fact which could only be attributed to the impression made on him by the debate, as he had previously made no secret of his non-concurrence in the proposal. The time appeared to my daughter, Miss Helen Taylor, to have come for forming a Society for the extension of the suffrage to women. The existence of the Society is due to my daughter's initiative; its constitution was planned entirely by her, and she was the soul of the movement during its first years, though delicate health and superabundant occupation made her decline to be a member of the Executive Committee. Many distinguished members of parliament, professors, and others, and some of the most eminent women of whom the country can boast, became members of the Society, a large proportion either directly or indirectly through my daughter's influence, she having written the greater number, and all the best, of the letters by which adhesions was obtained, even when those letters bore my signature. In two remarkable instances, those of Miss Nightingale and Miss Mary Carpenter, the reluctance those ladies had at first felt to come forward, (for it was not on their past difference of opinion) was overcome by appeals written by my daughter though signed by me. Associations for the same object were formed in various local centres, Manchester, Edinburgh, Birmingham, Bristol, and Glasgow; and others which have done much valuable work for the cause. All the Societies take the title of branches of the National Society for Women's Suffrage; but each has its own governing body, and acts in complete independence of the others.

I believe I have mentioned all that is worth remembering of my proceedings in the House. But their enumeration, even if complete, would give but an inadequate idea of my occupations during that period, and especially of the time taken up by correspondence. For many years before my election to Parliament, I had been continually receiving letters from strangers, mostly addressed to me as a writer on philosophy, and either propounding difficulties or communicating thoughts on subjects connected with logic or political economy. In common, I suppose, with all who are known as political economists, I was a recipient of all the shallow theories and absurd proposals by which people are perpetually endeavouring to show the way to universal wealth and happiness by some artful reorganization of the currency. When there were signs of sufficient intelligence in the writers to make it worth while attempting to put them right, I took the trouble to point out their errors, until the growth of my correspondence made it necessary to dismiss such persons with very brief answers. Many, however, of the communications I received were more worthy of attention than these, and in some, oversights of detail were pointed out in my writings, which I was thus enabled to correct. Correspondence of this sort naturally multiplied with the multiplication of the subjects on which I wrote, especially those of a metaphysical character. But when I became a member of parliament, I began to receive letters on private grievances and on every imaginable subject that related to any kind of public affairs, however remote from my knowledge or pursuits. It was not my constituents in Westminster who laid this burthen on me: they kept with remarkable fidelity the understanding on which I had consented to serve. I received, indeed, now and then an application from some ingenuous youth to procure for him a small government appointment; but these were few, and how simple and ignorant the writers were, was shown by the fact that the applications came in about equally whichever party was in power. My invariable answer was, that it was contrary to the principles on which I was elected to ask favours of any Government. But, on the whole, hardly any part of the country gave me less trouble than my own constituents. The general mass of correspondence, however, swelled into an oppressive burthen.

At this time, and thenceforth, a great proportion of all my letters (including many which found their way into the newspapers [1]) were not written by me but by my daughter; at first merely from her willingness to help in disposing of a mass of letters greater than I could get through without assistance, but afterwards because I thought the letters she wrote superior to mine, and more so in proportion to the difficulty and importance of the occasion. Even those which I wrote myself were generally much improved by her, as is also the case with all the more recent of my prepared speeches, of which, and of some of my published writings, not a few passages, and those the most successful, were hers.

While I remained in Parliament my work as an author was unavoidably limited to the recess. During that time I wrote (besides the pamphlet on Ireland, already mentioned), the Essay on Plato, published in the Edinburgh Review, and reprinted in the third volume of " Dissertations and Discussions; " and the Address which, conformably to custom, I delivered to the University of St. Andrew's, whose students had done me the honour of electing me to the office of Rector. In this Discourse I gave expression to many thoughts and opinions which had been accumulating in me through life, respecting the various studies which belong to a liberal education, their uses and influences, and the mode in which they should be pursued

---

[1] One which deserves particular mention is a letter respecting the Habitual Criminals Act and the functions of a police generally, written in answer to a private application for my opinion, but which got into the newspapers and excited some notice. This letter which was full of original and valuable thoughts was entirely my daughter's; the fertility and aptness which distinguishes her practical conceptions of the adaptation of means to ends is such as I can never hope to rival.

to render their influences most beneficial. The position I took up, vindicating the high educational value alike of the old classic and the new scientific studies, on even stronger grounds than are urged by most of their advocates, and insisting that it is only the stupid inefficiency of the usual teaching which makes those studies be regarded as competitors instead of allies, was, I think, calculated, not only to aid and stimulate the improvement which has happily commenced in the national institutions for higher education, but to diffuse juster ideas than we often find, even in highly educated men, on the conditions of the highest mental cultivation.

During this period also I commenced (and completed soon after I had left Parliament) the performance of a duty to philosophy and to the memory of my father, by preparing and publishing an edition of the " Analysis of the Phenomena of the Human Mind," with notes bringing up the doctrines of that admirable book to the latest improvements in science and in speculation. This was a joint undertaking: the psychological notes being furnished in about equal proportions by Mr. Bain and myself, while Mr. Grote supplied some valuable contributions on points in the history of philosophy incidentally raised, and Dr. Andrew Findlater supplied the deficiencies in the book which had been occasioned by the imperfect philological knowledge of the time when it was written. Having been originally published at a time when the current of metaphysical speculation ran in a quite opposite direction to the psychology of Experience and Association, the " Analysis " had not obtained the amount of immediate success which it deserved, though it had made a deep impression on many individual minds, and had largely contributed, through those minds, to create that more favourable atmosphere for the Association Psychology of which we now have the benefit. Admirably adapted for a class-book of the Experience Metaphysics, it only required to be enriched, and in

some cases corrected, by the results of more recent labours
in the same school of thought, to stand, as it now does, in
company with Mr. Bain's treatises, at the head of the
systematic works on Analytic psychology.

In the autumn of 1868 the Parliament which passed the
Reform Act was dissolved, and at the new election for
Westminster I was thrown out; not to my surprise, nor, I
believe, to that of my principal supporters, though in the
few days preceding the election they had become more
sanguine than before. That I should not have been elected
at all would not have required any explanation; what
excites curiosity is that I should have been elected the first
time, or, having been elected then, should have been defeated afterwards. But the efforts made to defeat me
were far greater on the second occasion than on the first.
For one thing, the Tory Government was now struggling
for existence, and success in any contest was of more importance to them. Then, too, all persons of Tory feelings
were far more embittered against me individually than on
the previous occasion; many who had at first been either
favourable or indifferent, were vehemently opposed to my
re-election. As I had shown in my political writings that
I was aware of the weak points in democratic opinions,
some Conservatives, it seems, had not been without hopes
of finding me an opponent of democracy: as I was able to
see the Conservative side of the question, they presumed
that, like them, I could not see any other side. Yet if
they had really read my writings, they would have known
that after giving full weight to all that appeared to me
well grounded in the arguments against democracy, I
unhesitatingly decided in its favour, while recommending
that it should be accompanied by such institutions as were
consistent with its principle and calculated to ward off
its inconveniences: one of the chief of these remedies being
Proportional Representation, on which scarcely any of the
Conservatives gave me any support. Some Tory expecta-

tions appear to have been founded on the approbation I
had expressed of plural voting, under certain conditions:
and it has been surmised that the suggestion of this sort
made in one of the Resolutions which Mr. Disraeli introduced into the House preparatory to his Reform Bill (a
suggestion which meeting with no favour he did not press),
may have been occasioned by what I had written on the
point: but if so, it was forgotten that I had made it an
express condition that the privilege of a plurality of votes
should be annexed to education, not to property, and even
so, had approved of it only on the supposition of universal
suffrage. How utterly inadmissible such plural voting
would be under the suffrage given by the present Reform
Act, is proved, to any who could otherwise doubt it, by
the very small weight which the working classes are found
to possess in elections, even under the law which gives no
more votes to any one elector than to any other.

While I thus was far more obnoxious to the Tory
interest, and to many Conservative Liberals than I had
formerly been, the course I pursued in Parliament had by
no means been such as to make Liberals generally at all
enthusiastic in my support. It has already been mentioned, how large a proportion of my prominent appearances had been on questions on which I differed from most
of the Liberal party, or about which they cared little, and
how few occasions there had been on which the line I took
was such as could lead them to attach any great value to
me as an organ of their opinions. I had moreover done
things which had excited, in many minds, a personal prejudice against me. Many were offended by what they called
the persecution of Mr. Eyre: and still greater offence was
taken at my sending a subscription to the election expenses
of Mr. Bradlaugh. Having refused to be at any expense
for my own election, and having had all its expenses de-
frayed by others, I felt under a peculiar obligation to subscribe in my turn where funds were deficient for candi-

dates whose election was desirable. I accordingly sent
subscriptions to nearly all the working class candidates, and
among others to Mr. Bradlaugh. He had the support of
the working classes; having heard him speak, I knew him
to be a man of ability, and he had proved that he was the
reverse of a demagogue, by placing himself in strong
opposition to the prevailing opinion of the democratic party
on two such important subjects as Malthusianism and
Personal Representation. Men of this sort, who, while
sharing the democratic feelings of the working classes,
judged political questions for themselves, and had courage
to assert their individual convictions against popular opposition, were needed, as it seemed to be, in Parliament, and
I did not think that Mr. Bradlaugh's anti-religious opinions (even though he had been intemperate in the expression of them) ought to exclude him. In subscribing,
however, to his election, I did what would have been highly
imprudent if I had been at liberty to consider only the
interests of my own re-election; and, as might be expected,
the utmost possible use, both fair and unfair, was made
of this act of mine to stir up the electors of Westminster
against me. To these various causes, combined with an
unscrupulous use of the usual pecuniary and other influences
on the side of my Tory competitor, while none were used
on my side, it is to be ascribed that I failed at my second
election after having succeeded at the first. No sooner
was the result of the election known than I received three
or four invitations to become a candidate for other constituencies, chiefly counties; but even if success could have
been expected, and this without expense, I was not disposed
to deny myself the relief of returning to private life. I
had no cause to feel humiliated at my rejection by the
electors; and if I had, the feeling would have been far
outweighed by the numerous expressions of regret which
I received from all sorts of persons and places, and in a
most marked degree from those members of the liberal

party in Parliament, with whom I had been accustomed to act.

Since that time little has occurred which there is need to commemorate in this place. I returned to my old pursuits and to the enjoyment of a country life in the South of Europe, alternating twice a year with a residence of some weeks or months in the neighbourhood of London. I have written various articles in periodicals (chiefly in my friend Mr. Morley's Fortnightly Review), have made a small number of speeches on public occasions, especially at the meetings of the Women's Suffrage Society, have published the "Subjection of Women," written some years before, with some additions by my daughter and myself, and have commenced the preparation of matter for future books, of which it will be time to speak more particularly if I live to finish them. Here, therefore, for the present, this Memoir may close.

INDEX[1]

Abolitionists. *See* United States, civil war

Æschines, early study of, 8

Æsop's Fables, study of, 4

Aldrich, study of his logic, 85

Algebra, early study of, 7–8

America. *See* United States

Amusements, lack of in boyhood, 25–26

Anacreon, early study of, 8

Analysis, effect on the feelings, 96–101

Analytic psychology. *See* Psychology

Annual register, early reading of, 5

Anson's *Voyage*, 6

Anthology, early study of, 8

Arabian nights, 6

Aristocratic rule, James Mill's opinions on, 65, 74–75; J. S. Mill's opinions on, 120–121

Aristophanes, early study of, 8

Aristotle, *Rhetoric*, early study of, 8; *Organon, Analytics*, etc., 12–13

Arithmetic, early study of, 4

Association, principle of, 75, 217; source of all feelings and qualities, 95–96; and Sir William Hamilton's philosophy, 191–194

Atheism, James Mill's opinion of, 28

Athenian institutions, 14–15

Austin, Charles, friendship with, 54–56; contributor to the *Westminster review*, 67–68; utilitarian propagandism, 72; ed. of Marshall's *Parliamentary history and review*, 82–83; Owenites, 87; Cambridge union, 88; London debating society, 88

Austin, John, study of law under, 45; friendship with, 51–53; contributor to the *Westminster review*, 67–68; change of opinions under German influence, 124–126; enemy to Parliamentary reform, 182; *Lectures on Jurisprudence*, 190

Authors' signatures to articles in periodicals, 140

Axioms in ratiocination, 127

Bailey's *Dissertation on value*, study of, 84

Baillie, Joanna, 11 footnote

Bain, influence on Mill's *System of logic*, 174 footnote; intuitional philosophy, 192; assisting in a new ed. of James Mill's *Analysis of the phenomena of the human mind*, 217–218

Baldwin, publisher, and the *Westminster review*, 66

Ballot. *See* Suffrage

Baring, Alexander, petition for free trade, 69

Barrow Green House, Bentham's home, visits to, 38

Beattie, early study of, 11

Beauchamp, Philip (pseud.), study of, 49–50

Beaver's *African memoranda*, 6

Belper, Lord (Strutt), acquaintance with, 54; utilitarian propagandism, 72; contributor to the *Parliamentary history and review*, 83; Reformed parliament, 136

Bentham, Jeremy, V; books borrowed from, 5; friendship with, 38–39; practice of making marginal notes, 44; and John Austin, 45; principles of morality, 45–46; *Traité*

---

[1] Prepared by Mary Leslie Irwin and Mortimer J. Adler, Columbia University.